LEGEND
DARK HORSE COMICS
SIN CITY
3 OF 6
$2.95 US
$4.00 CAN
A DAME TO KILL

CREATED, WRITTEN, & DRAWN BY

FRANK MILLER

Editor
DIANA SCHUTZ

Assistant Editor
AARON WALKER

Design & Production
CARY GRAZZINI

Publisher
MIKE RICHARDSON

This volume collects issues one through six of the Dark Horse comic book series *Sin City®: A Dame to Kill For*, originally edited by Jerry Prosser and published between November 1993 and May 1994.

Published by Dark Horse Books
A division of Dark Horse Comics, Inc.
10956 SE Main Street
Milwaukie, Oregon 97222

DarkHorse.com

Second hardcover edition: June 2014
ISBN 978-1-61655-239-8

1 3 5 7 9 10 8 6 4 2
Printed in China

FRANK MILLER
A DAME TO KILL FOR
A TALE FROM
SIN CITY®
DARK HORSE BOOKS®

CHAPTER ONE

IT'S ANOTHER HOT NIGHT, DRY AND WINDLESS. THE KIND THAT MAKES PEOPLE DO SWEATY, SECRET THINGS.
I WAIT AND I LISTEN.
FOR A WHILE IT'S AS QUIET AS IT GETS IN SIN CITY. COYOTE CALLS FROM THE HILLS. POLICE SIRENS, RISING, FALLING, CUTTING THROUGH THE TRAFFIC'S WHITE-NOISE ROAR.
MY RIGHT CALF IS BEGINNING TO CRAMP UP AND I'M THINKING ABOUT GOING DOWNSTAIRS AND GETTING MY MONEY BACK FROM THE BELLHOP WHEN I HEAR THE JANGLE OF KEYS AT THE DOOR AND THEY COME IN...
THIS IS THE LAST TIME, SALLY. IT'S GOT TO BE THE LAST TIME.

CLICK!
WHAT-EVER YOU SAY, JOEY.
I MEAN IT, THIS TIME.
SHE GLIDES OUT OF HER COAT LIKE IT WAS CHRISTMAS WRAPPING, PLAYING IT FOR ALL IT'S WORTH. AND IT'S WORTH PLENTY. SHE'S GOT THE KIND OF FIGURE YOU NOTICE.
IT'S HER VOICE THAT SPOILS EVERYTHING.

CLICK!
A LITTLE GIRL'S VOICE, ALL SQUEAKY AND MOUSY AND BUBBLY AND BOUNCY WITH FALSE INNOCENCE...
I HAD A DREAM ABOUT YOU LAST NIGHT, JOEY. IT WAS A NICE DREAM. DO YOU WANT TO HEAR ABOUT IT?

NO. NO DREAMS TONIGHT. I HAVEN'T GOT THE TIME. I HAVEN'T GOT ANY TIME. I HAVE TO GET HOME. SOON. AND THIS IS THE END FOR US. THE LAST TIME. I CAN'T GO ON TAKING THE CHANCE.
WHATEVER *YOU* SAY, JOEY. *YOU* GIVE THE ORDERS. *YOU'RE* THE BOSS.
SHE ADDS A GOOD HALF-DOZEN EXTRA SYLLABLES TO *"BOSS,"* ENDING IT WITH A THROUGH-THE-TEETH HISS THAT'S ALL BUSINESS.
AND ALREADY HE'S BREATHING HARD, THE JERK.

CLICK!
IT'S GLORIA, DAMN HER. SHE'S ASKING ALL KINDS OF QUESTIONS. SHE SUSPECTS SOMETHING. SHE'LL SUE. SHE'LL GET EVERY-THING.

EVERY-THING YOU'VE WORKED SO HARD FOR.
YOU'RE DAMN RIGHT I WORK HARD. I WORK MY BUTT OFF. NIGHT AND DAY. I ALWAYS HAVE. BUILT MY BUSINESS UP OUT OF NOTHING. NOTHING.
AND NOBODY APPRECIATES YOU, DO THEY, JOEY? NOT LIKE YOU DESERVE.
NO. NOBODY. NOT THE EMPLOYEES I KEEP OFF FOOD STAMPS--AND NOT GLORIA, DAMN HER. MY OWN WIFE. LIVING IN THAT HOUSE I BOUGHT HER. WEARING THOSE CLOTHES I BOUGHT HER. WITH MY MONEY. MY HARD-EARNED MONEY. AND SHE DOESN'T APPRECIATE A DAMN THING.

SHE DOESN'T EVEN TRY TO UNDERSTAND THE KIND OF PRESSURE I'M UNDER. SHE DOESN'T EVEN TRY. DAMN HER. SHE'S ALWAYS COMING AT ME. ALWAYS MAKING DEMANDS. NEVER GIVING ME A BREAK. JUST LIKE ALL THOSE LAZY BUMS WHO WOULDN'T HAVE A PAYCHECK IF I DIDN'T SIGN IT -- THEY CAN GET SICK, BUT ME? *NOT A CHANCE!*

IT'S BECAUSE YOU'RE SO STRONG.
YOU'RE DAMN RIGHT ABOUT THAT! BUT DO I GET ANY CREDIT? HELL, NO! THEY JUST TAKE AND TAKE!

ONE OF THESE DAYS I'LL FIRE THE WHOLE PACK OF THEM! SHOW THEM WHO'S THE BIG MAN! SHOW THEM WHO'S BOSS!
YOU CAN SHOW *ME*, JOEY.

CHINK
K
YOU CAN SHOW ME WHO'S BOSS.

SNAP
I WILL...
SNAP

I'LL SHOW YOU... I'LL SHOW YOU WHO'S BOSS...

THEN SHE'S MOANING AND SAYING "BOSS" IN TIME WITH HIS GRUNTS. IT'S ALL OVER PRETTY QUICKLY.
CLICK! CLICK! CLICK!
I GET EVERYTHING I NEED.
THE SAD THING IS THAT SOME OF THE COMPOSITIONS I PICK ARE PRETTY GOOD.
OH, GOD, JOEY. THAT WAS JUST INCREDIBLE. YOU MAKE ME FEEL LIKE A WOMAN. I KNOW THAT SOUNDS CORNY, BUT IT'S TRUE. SO TRUE.
IT TAKES A REAL MAN TO MAKE A GIRL FEEL LIKE THIS.
I LOVE YOU, BABY. YOU KNOW I LOVE YOU.

I LOVE YOU TOO, JOEY. YOU'RE ALL THE MAN I'LL EVER NEED. I COUNT THE MINUTES, WHEN YOU'RE GONE. I HONESTLY DO.
MY WRISTS HURT, JOEY. THINK YOU COULD GET THE KEYS? THEY'RE RIGHT IN MY PURSE.
YOU DON'T HAVE ANY IDEA HOW MUCH I LOVE YOU. HOW MUCH I'VE SACRIFICED. IT'S TEARING ME UP INSIDE...
JOEY-- WHAT ARE YOU *DOING?!*
IT'S TEARING ME UP! HOW MUCH I LOVE YOU--AND WHAT I HAVE TO DO! BUT I'VE WORKED HARD! DAMN HARD! AND GLORIA WOULD GET EVERYTHING! IT'S ALL HER FAULT! I DON'T HAVE ANY CHOICE!

JOEY. NO. PLEASE. I WON'T TELL ANYBODY. I SWEAR TO GOD.
I KNOW YOU WON'T *WANT* TO TALK, SALLY. I KNOW THAT...
OH, MY ACHING BACK...
...BUT YOU'RE ONLY HUMAN. AND GLORIA WILL OFFER A LOT OF MONEY. MY MONEY. MY OWN MONEY AND SHE'LL USE IT TO BRING ME DOWN...
I'LL GO AWAY. I'LL LEAVE TOWN AND GO SOMEPLACE SHE'LL NEVER FIND ME.
YEAH? AND HOW WILL YOU GET THERE? FLY? AND WHO WILL PAY FOR THE TICKET? THE TICKET AND GOD KNOWS WHAT ELSE! AN APARTMENT? A CAR? CLOTHES? YOU'LL SUCK ME DRY AND YOU'LL NEVER STOP!

KASHHHHH
JOEY-- I BEG YOU, BABY...
DON'T MAKE THIS ANY HARDER THAN IT IS, DAMN YOU!
YAAA

KILL HIM!
KILL HIM!
WHUD
BLAGG

NOBODY'S KILLING ANYBODY. NOT WHILE I'M AROUND.

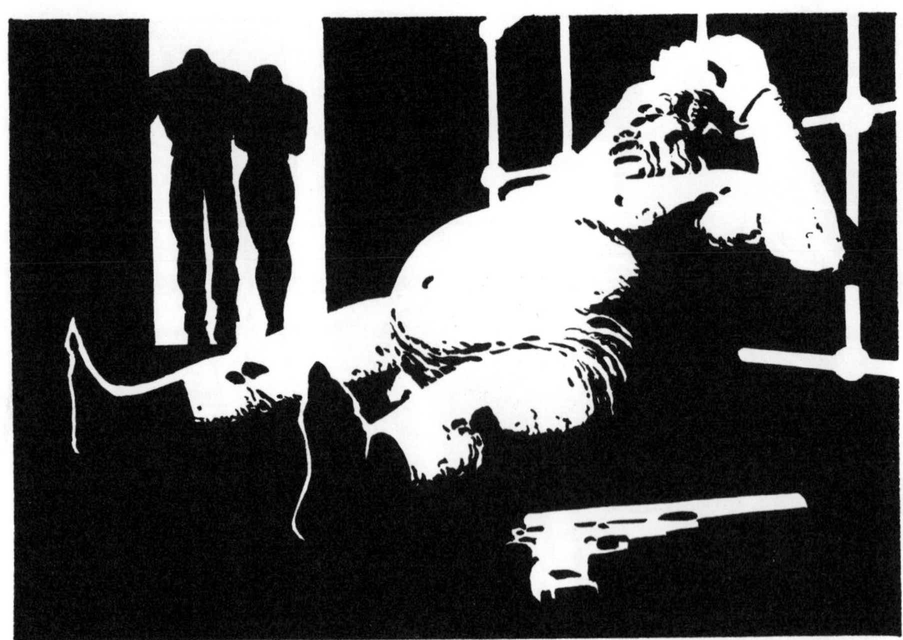

"THEN CAN I HAVE A RIDE?" SHE ASKS, USING HER REAL VOICE THIS TIME, A VOICE THAT'S LEFT INNOCENCE A LIFETIME BEHIND.

I GRAB THE KEYS AND UNCUFF HER. I LEAVE THE JERK FOR HOUSE-KEEPING.

ON THE WAY OUT SHE GIVES HIM A KICK THAT'LL STILL HURT LIKE HELL WHEN HE COMES TO.

I TAKE REDONDO OVER THE HILL, TOWARD OLD TOWN. IT TAKES LONGER THAT WAY, BUT I FIGURE WITH THE WAY SHE'S SHAKING SHE COULD USE THE TIME TO SETTLE DOWN. AT FIRST ALL SHE CAN DO IS SOB AND BLOW HER NOSE AND SMOKE CIGARETTES.

SHE SMOKES SIX CIGARETTES.

SHE'S JUST ABOUT PULLED HERSELF TOGETHER WHEN SOME CRAZY BLONDE CUTS US OFF, MAKING POOR SALLY ALMOST JUMP OUT OF HER SKIN.

DRIVING LIKE A BAT OUT OF HELL, THAT ONE.

CRAZY.

THERE'S NEVER A GOOD REASON FOR BREAKING THE SPEED LIMIT.

THE LAST I SEE OF SALLY, SHE'S FIXED HER MAKEUP AND SHE'S SAUNTERING AWAY LIKE A PRO, TOSSING ME A WAVE AND A WINK, ONE HOOKER TO ANOTHER.

THEN SHE BLENDS INTO THE SEA OF FLESH THAT IS OLD TOWN.

OLD TOWN. WHERE BEAUTY IS CHEAP, PROVIDED ALL YOU WANT TO DO IS LOOK.

BUT IF YOU'RE READY TO PAY, YOU CAN HAVE ANYTHING YOU CAN IMAGINE.

I HOLD TIGHT TO THE WHEEL TO KEEP MY HANDS FROM SHAKING. I PULL OUT AND CUT BACK OVER THE HILL. OUT. AWAY.

I PUT THE GAME ON AND PRAY IT WILL CHASE AWAY THE MEMORIES. THE DAMN OLD TOWN MEMORIES, OF DRUNKEN MORNINGS AND SWEATY SEX AND STUPID, BLOODY BRAWLS.

YOU CAN'T JUST PICK AND CHOOSE. YOU CAN'T TAKE THE GOOD WITHOUT THE BAD.

NOT ONCE YOU LET THE MONSTER OUT.

THE TEAM'S UP BY TWELVE LATE IN THE THIRD WHEN I PULL UP TO AGAMEMNON'S. I SHOULD BE HOME IN TIME TO CATCH THE FOURTH-QUARTER REPLAY AT ELEVEN.

AGAMEMNON'S EATING, LIKE ALWAYS. AND HE'S CHEERFUL, ALSO LIKE ALWAYS.

IT'S AGAMEMNON WHO GOT ME INTO THESE MARITAL JOBS. IT'S HIS SPECIALTY. HE TOSSES ME WORK HE CAN'T HANDLE BECAUSE HE'S SO FAT. HE KEEPS HALF THE MONEY, WHICH I THINK IS FAIR, CONSIDERING I GET TO USE HIS DARKROOM UNTIL I CAN AFFORD MY OWN EQUIPMENT. WHICH I HOPE IS SOON, BECAUSE EVEN THOUGH I'M GRATEFUL TO THE GUY FOR THE WORK, AGAMEMNON MAKES ME SICK.

THE CANELLI JOB? GOD DAMN! I KNEW THAT BUM COULDN'T KEEP IT IN HIS PANTS MUCH LONGER!
YOU CATCH THE GAME? OUR BOY GABRIEL IS KICKING BUTT!
YEAH. THE BLUES MIGHT JUST GO ALL THE WAY, THIS YEAR.
I'M HOPING TO CATCH THE REPLAY AT ELEVEN.
KISS ME I'M GREEK
IF I HAD TO NAIL IT DOWN, I'D SAY THE MAIN REASON AGAMEMNON MAKES ME SICK IS HOW MUCH HE LOVES HIS JOB.
OH, YEAH... OH, BOY... OH, YEAH ... YOU'RE A GENIUS, KID... OH, YEAH... GOD, JUST LOOK AT THEM...

...WILL YOU GET A LOAD OF THOSE *HOOTERS?* STRAIGHT OUT OF *PLAYBOY MAGAZINE!* AND KNOWING YOU, YOU DIDN'T GET YOURSELF A PIECE OF THAT, DID YOU? NAH, NOT *CLEAN LIVER.* NOT THE *BOY SCOUT.*

HANDCUFFS. IT'S FUNNY, *YOU* KNOW. HOW MANY OF THEM GO FOR THE HANDCUFFS. ESPECIALLY THE BUSINESSMEN. AND JUDGES, TOO. YOU WOULDN'T BELIEVE HOW MANY JUDGES GO FOR THE CUFFS.

SOME OF THEM LIKE THE GALS TO WEAR THEM, AND SOME LIKE TO PUT THEM ON THEMSELVES. I TELL YA, I COULD WRITE A BOOK...

MAYBE TOMORROW I'LL GO TO THE TIMES AND CRAWL ON MY BELLY AND BEG GILLERAN FOR MY OLD JOB BACK. MAYBE HE'LL GIVE ME A BREAK. HE SAID I DESERVED A PULITZER, ONCE.
BUT THAT WAS THEN.

I DRIVE TEN BLOCKS OUT OF MY WAY AND STOP FOR GAS I DON'T NEED, SCREWING UP MY COURAGE FOR THE WORST OF IT.
-- THE WIFE.
THIS ONE'S GOT A LAWYER TO PAY THE TAB AND DO THE TALKING, SO IT'S EASIER.
...IN CASH, AS YOU REQUESTED. YOU MAY BE CALLED UPON FOR A DEPOSITION. PLEASE LEAVE BY THE SIDE EXIT.

THE MUSTANG SHUDDERS, ANGRY, ACTING LIKE THE WILD HORSE IT WAS NAMED AFTER, BEGGING TO CUT LOOSE AND SHOW WHAT IT CAN DO.
I DON'T LET IT.
I'VE GOT THE RADIO TUNED TO SOME LONELY HEARTS TALK SHOW, BUT I'M NOT LISTENING. ONE MORE TIME, I SORT THROUGH THE BROKEN PIECES OF MY PAST. AND LIKE ALWAYS, THEY COME TOGETHER TO FORM THE SAME, SORRY PICTURE.
I THINK ABOUT ALL THE WAYS I'VE SCREWED UP AND WHAT I'D GIVE FOR ONE CLEAR CHANCE TO WIPE THE SLATE CLEAN. TO DIG MY WAY OUT OF THE NUMB, GRAY HELL I'VE MADE OF MY LIFE.
I'D GIVE ANYTHING.
JUST TO CUT LOOSE. JUST TO FEEL THE FIRE. ONE MORE TIME.

VROOM!

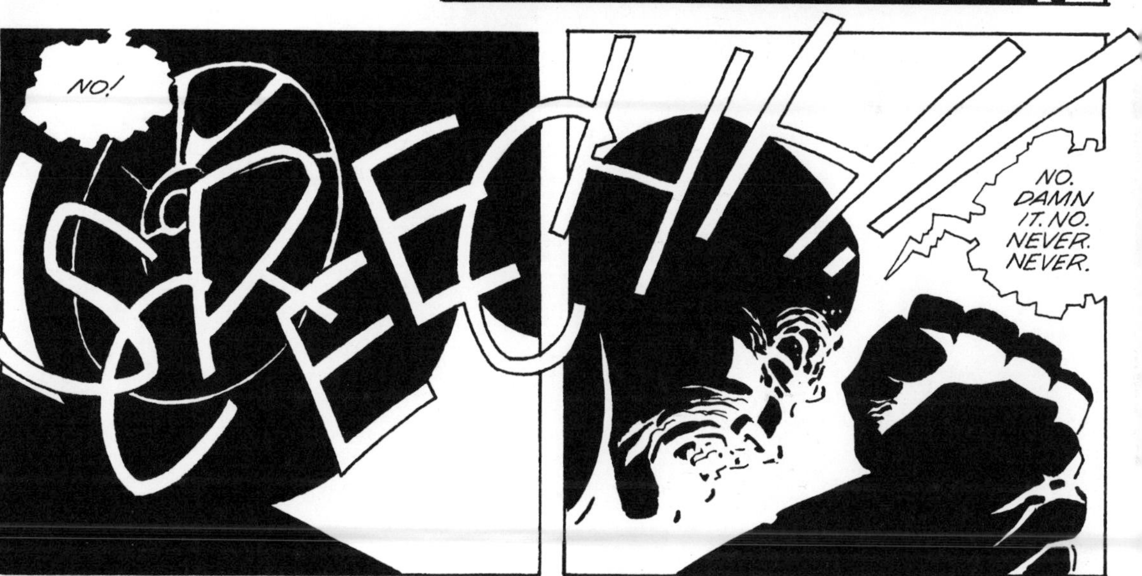
NO!
SCREECHH!
NO. DAMN IT. NO. NEVER. NEVER.

NEVER LOSE CONTROL. NOT FOR ONE SECOND. NEVER.
NEVER LET THE MONSTER OUT.

CHAPTER TWO

FOURTH-QUARTER REPLAY.
--AND IT'S DONNER ON A FAST BREAK --AND THERE'S GABRIEL WITH A STEAL --WHAT A STEAL! --TEARING UP COURT--HE SHOOTS--FOULED HARD-- IT NEEDS A BOUNCE-- YES!
SCORE!
302
302
RING!

--AND THEY'RE CALLING A FLAGRANT FOUL ON MARK DONNER! THAT'S IT! HE'S OUT OF THERE!
GABRIEL SHOOTS THE FOUL-- YES!
SCORE!
RING!

HELLO?
THIS ONE'S HISTORY, FOLKS...

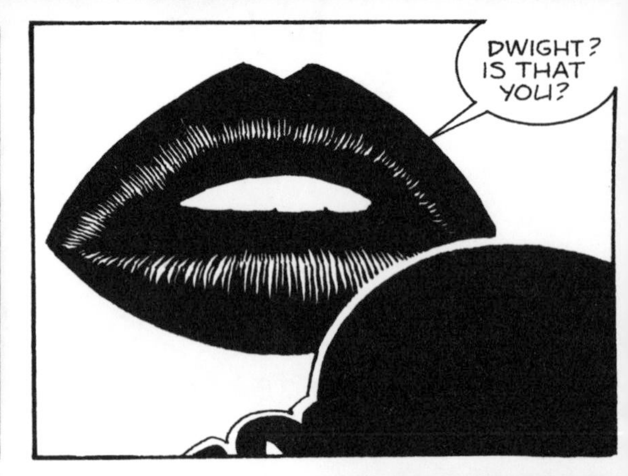
DWIGHT? IS THAT YOU?

AVA.

I'M SORRY TO CALL. I KNOW I'VE GOT NO RIGHT. BUT I NEED TO SEE YOU. TONIGHT. PLEASE, DWIGHT. DON'T HANG UP. PLEASE.

SHE KEEPS TALKING.
AND LIKE AN IDIOT, I KEEP LISTENING.

AVA.
DAMN.

I SHOULD TELL HER TO GO TO HELL. INSTEAD, I GIVE MYSELF A SHAVE I DON'T NEED AND I SHOW UP TWENTY MINUTES EARLY.
AVA. DAMN.
WHAT THE HELL COULD SHE WANT WITH ME NOW?
CLUB PECOS
HE'D DESERVE IT...
GLAKK
SURE, BILL. LET'S GET YOU HOME.
YOU CAN'T DRIVE TWO BLOCKS IN SIN CITY WITHOUT COMING ACROSS A SALOON. THIS ONE'S A COUNTRY JOINT, THE BAD KIND.
IT'S NOT THE KIND OF PLACE I'D EXPECT HER TO KNOW ABOUT, LET ALONE GO TO.

I GRAB MYSELF ONE LAST LUNGFUL OF NIGHT AIR. THEN I TRADE IT IN FOR A SMOKY SOUP SPICED WITH SWEAT AND VOMIT AND BOOZE AND BLOOD.
I KNOW THE FLAVOR WELL.
HOW'S IT GOING, MARV?
YOU KNOW, DWIGHT. SAME OLD, SAME OLD.

HAVEN'T SEEN YOU IN A DOG'S AGE, PAL. YOU BEEN OUT OF TOWN?
NO, JUST BUSY. YOU TAKE CARE, MARV.
MARV'S A GUY YOU'VE GOT TO BE CAREFUL AROUND. HE DOESN'T MEAN ANY HARM, BUT HE CAUSES PLENTY.
THE POOR SLOB. JUST ANOTHER LOSER IN A JOINT THAT'S FULL OF THEM.
WHY HERE, AVA? IT'S NOT LIKE YOU. NO, WITH YOU EVERYTHING ALWAYS HAD TO BE FIRST CLASS. ALL THE WAY.
AND WHEN I COULDN'T FOOT THE BILL, YOU SURE AS HELL FOUND SOMEBODY WHO COULD.

I ORDER UP A GINGER ALE AND STARE AT IT FOR THE BETTER PART OF AN HOUR.
SHE'S LATE, LIKE SHE ALWAYS WAS.

AND LIKE ALWAYS, SHE'S WORTH THE WAIT.

DWIGHT... HOW LONG HAS IT BEEN? FOUR YEARS?
SOUNDS ABOUT RIGHT. HAVE A SEAT.

SHE ASKS FOR SOME KIND OF SCOTCH NOBODY'S EVER HEARD OF, THEN SETTLES FOR WHAT THEY HAVE.
NOT LIKE HER TO DRINK HARD STUFF. THE CIGARETTES ARE A SURPRISE, TOO. USED TO BE SHE COULDN'T STAND THE SMELL OF THEM.
SO MANY TIMES I'VE WANTED TO CALL YOU. I'VE FOUND MYSELF THINKING ABOUT YOU...
I'VE GOT PLACES TO BE. HOW ABOUT YOU JUST TELL ME WHAT YOU WANT.

SHE MOVES CLOSE, ALL VULNERABLE, A DEER CAUGHT IN THE HEADLIGHTS.
I COULD SLUG HER.
DON'T BE COLD, DWIGHT. I DON'T THINK I COULD STAND THAT, RIGHT NOW. I MUST STILL MEAN SOMETHING TO YOU. YOU CAME HERE. YOU MUST STILL CARE. JUST A LITTLE BIT.
SURE. YOU CALLED AND I CAME RUNNING. YOU'VE STILL GOT THAT MUCH OF A HOLD ON ME AND MAYBE YOU ALWAYS WILL. BUT I'VE GOT NO REASON AT ALL TO BE NICE ABOUT IT. NOT AFTER WHAT YOU DID TO ME.
I GUESS I DESERVED THAT.
THERE'S NO GUESSING TO IT. YOU DESERVE THAT AND A WHOLE LOT MORE. YOU DON'T KNOW WHAT I WENT THROUGH. HOW BAD IT GOT.
MAYBE IF YOU'D FALLEN IN LOVE WITH THE SLOB I COULD'VE HANDLED IT.
BUT YOU DIDN'T LOVE HIM. YOU'VE NEVER LOVED ANYBODY. MONEY WAS ALL YOU WERE AFTER. YOU TOSSED ME AWAY-- FOR *CASH*.
SO LET'S NOT SCREW AROUND. I'M HERE. I'M LISTENING. YOU JUST TELL ME WHAT THE HELL IT IS YOU WANT.
THERE'S ONLY ONE THING I WANT FROM YOU! AND I WANT IT SO DESPERATELY I COULD SCREAM! I WANT YOU TO FORGIVE ME!

OH. NOW I GET IT. YOU'VE GOT A CONSCIENCE, AFTER ALL. AND IT'S BUGGING YOU.
FINE. YOU'RE FORGIVEN. YOU GOT YOUR WISH. GO HOME. SLEEP TIGHT.
YOU'RE RIGHT ABOUT ME! I'M NOTHING BUT A SELFISH SLUT WHO THREW AWAY THE ONLY MAN SHE EVER LOVED! JUST LIKE YOU SAID! BUT I WAS WRONG, DARLING! WRONG!
I'M IN HELL, DWIGHT. IT'S WORSE THAN YOU CAN IMAGINE... OH, GOD... I WISH I COULD GO BACK IN TIME. BACK TO THE WAY IT WAS. TO YOU AND ME. I'M SUCH A FOOL. SUCH A SELFISH, STUPID SLUT...
YOU MADE YOUR BED. SLEEP IN IT.
FORGIVE ME, DARLING. I BEG YOU. I LOVE YOU.

YOU DO THAT AGAIN AND I SWEAR TO HELL I'LL KILL YOU.

IF YOU CAN'T FORGIVE ME, DARLING, THEN PLEASE -- REMEMBER ME. THEY SAY YOU NEVER REALLY DIE AS LONG AS SOMEBODY REMEMBERS YOU.
WHAT THE DEVIL ARE YOU TALKING ABOUT?
MRS. LORD, YOU ARE DUE AT HOME.

SHE GASPS AND GRABS MY ARM AND SUDDENLY I'M PLAYING LANCELOT.
I'D SAY THAT'S UP TO MRS. LORD.
THIS IS NONE OF YOUR CONCERN, SIR.
IS THAT CLOWN GIVING YOU A HARD TIME, DWIGHT?
I'LL TAKE HIM DOWN FOR YOU IF YOU WANT. I GOT NOTHING GOING TONIGHT.
URPP

NEVER MIND, DWIGHT. IT'S TOO LATE. I'LL GO WITH HIM.
TOO LATE FOR WHAT, AVA?

FOR EVERYTHING.
JUST REMEMBER ME, MY LOVE. REMEMBER ME.

BUDDY, I DON'T MEAN TO POKE MY NOSE IN WHERE IT DON'T BELONG, BUT THAT THERE IS A DAME TO KILL FOR. WHY'D YOU LET HER *GO?*
THE NIGHT AIR HASN'T GOTTEN ANY COLDER.
IT JUST FEELS THAT WAY.
AVA.
DAMN!

CHAPTER THREE

THE NEXT DAY GOES BY ALL RIGHT. I KEEP DISTRACTED. I PAY MY RENT AND ROTATE MY TIRES. I GO SEE THREE MOVIES. I DON'T THINK ABOUT AVA TOO OFTEN.

THEN NIGHT FALLS AND THERE'S NOWHERE TO HIDE. THERE'S NO GAME ON, NOBODY TO CALL. I TRY TO READ BUT IT JUST WON'T HAPPEN.

SO I GET INTO BED AND CLOSE MY EYES AND REMIND MYSELF ABOUT ALL THE REASONS WHY I SHOULDN'T GIVE A DAMN ABOUT AVA. IT DOESN'T WORK. THE WRONG MEMORIES KEEP POPPING UP.

SHE RIPPED MY SOUL APART AND TOSSED AWAY THE PIECES LIKE SHE WAS EMPTYING AN ASHTRAY. BUT DOES MY MIND STAY ON THAT? HELL, NO! IT BRINGS BACK THAT LOOK SHE HAD IN HER EYES WHEN I TOLD HER ABOUT MY DAD. THAT TIME WE SMOKED POT AND GOT THE GIGGLES AND COULDN'T STOP. THAT CRAZY WAY SHE GOT SCARED IN THE MIDDLE OF THE NIGHT AND STARTED CRYING AND HOW I HELD HER CLOSE TO ME UNTIL DAWN.

AND YEAH, I REMEMBER THE FIRE IN HER, THE FEEL OF HER BREASTS, THE TASTE SHE LEFT IN MY MOUTH.

AVA.

WHAT AM I DOING *SMOKING?*
WHERE DID I GET THESE *CIGARETTES?*

NEVER GIVE AN INCH. NEVER. NEVER LET THE MONSTER OUT.
IT'S AVA. MAKING YOU CRAZY, ALL OVER AGAIN.

SHAKE HER OFF. FORGET HER. WHATEVER SHE'S IN FOR, SHE DESERVES IT.
BUT DOES SHE DESERVE TO DIE? THAT'S WHAT SHE SAID. THAT SHE WAS GOING TO DIE.
MAYBE IT'S ALL A PACK OF LIES. SOME SICK JOKE SHE'S PULLING ON ME FOR THE SHEER CRUELTY OF IT.
I HAVE TO KNOW, ONE WAY OR THE OTHER.
I HAVE TO KNOW.

IT SHOULDN'T TAKE TOO MUCH EFFORT TO GET TO THE BOTTOM OF THIS. JUST A SIMPLE JOB OF BREAKING AND ENTERING, PUNISHABLE BY UP TO FIVE YEARS IN THE SLAMMER, IF I'M CAUGHT.

IT TAKES A HALF HOUR TO CLIMB THE HILL OUT OF SIN CITY, UP TO WHERE THE AIR BLOWS COOL AND THE RICH FOLKS LIVE.

AND THEY DON'T GET MUCH RICHER THAN DAMIEN LORD. THE GUY DINES WITH ROARKS AND ROCKEFELLERS.

DAMIEN LORD.

AVA'S HUSBAND.

MY TELESCOPIC LENS LETS ME HAVE A LOOK AROUND.
I WIND UP SEEING A LOT MORE OF AVA THAN I BARGAINED FOR.

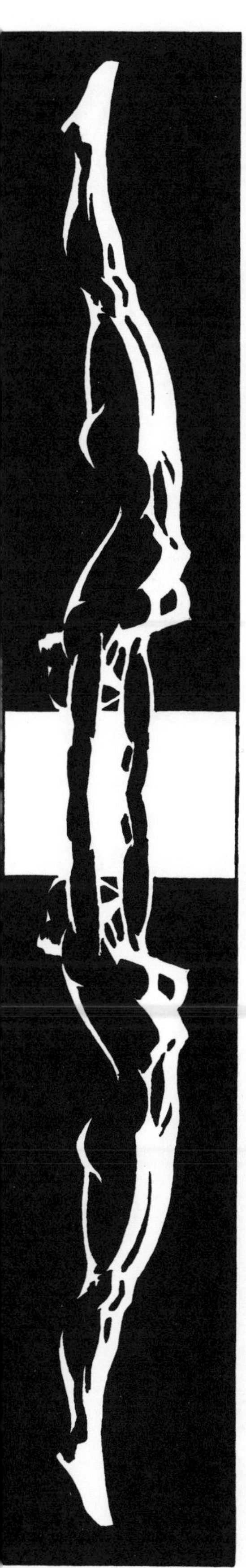

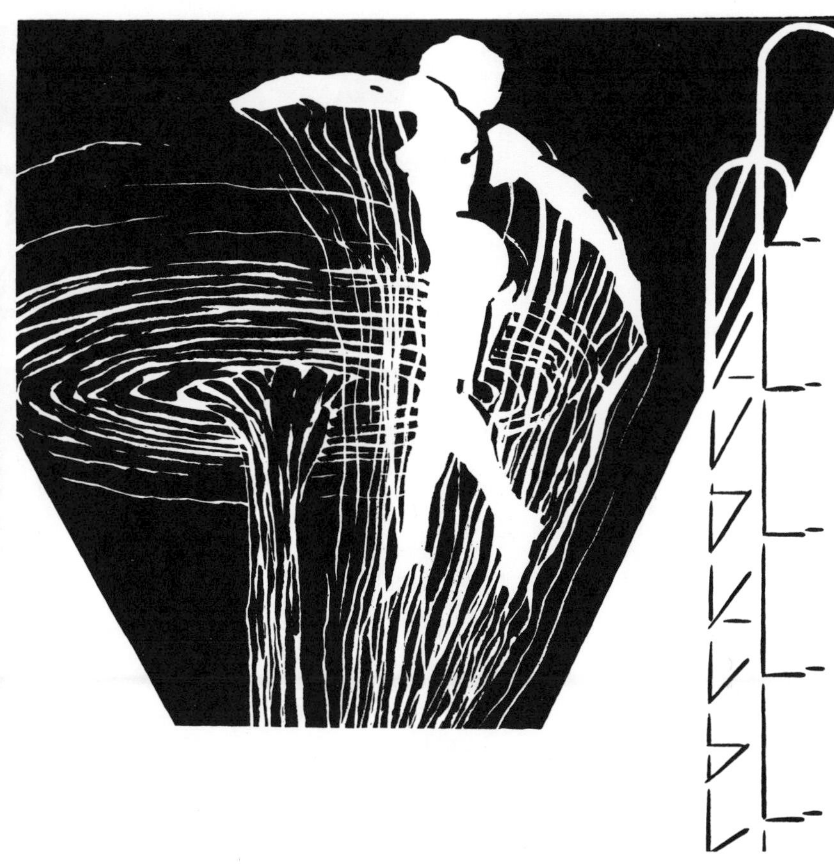

AVA MAY HAVE PICKED UP A FEW BAD HABITS, OVER THE YEARS--
--BUT SHE'S SURE AS HELL KEPT IN SHAPE.

FREEZE, PERVERT!
DON'T MOVE A MUSCLE!

I SAID FREEZE!
BREKK
YAAAAA

OOF!
YAAAAAAA

LET ME *THROUGH*, KOONTZ!
I'M SORRY, MA'AM. HE MIGHT BE ARMED.
I MUST ASK *YOU* WHAT *YOU* ARE DOING HERE, SIR.
MAKING A TOTAL ASS OF MYSELF.
HE WAS TAKING PICTURES OF MRS. LORD, THE *PERVERT*.
THE BIG GUY--IT WAS HIM WHO TOOK AVA AWAY FROM THE SALOON. BUT HE DOESN'T SEEM TO RECOGNIZE ME.
BETTER LET THEM THINK I'M JUST A PEEPING TOM. WHATEVER TROUBLE AVA'S IN, I DON'T WANT TO MAKE IT WORSE.

A DOOR SLIDES OPEN WITH A WHISPER. DAMIEN LORD LOOKS ME OVER LIKE I'M SOMETHING THAT FELL OUT OF THE BACK END OF A HORSE. WHICH IS PRETTY MUCH HOW I FEEL ABOUT MYSELF RIGHT THIS MINUTE.
AND WHAT DO WE HAVE HERE, MANUTE?
AN INTRUDER, SIR. A *VOYEUR*, BY ALL APPEARANCES. RATHER PATHETIC, DON'T *YOU* THINK?
I LIKE TO TAKE PICTURES.

I KNOW IT'S WRONG. I'M GETTING HELP. BUT SOMETIMES I CAN'T STOP MYSELF. I DON'T HURT ANYBODY.

WE NEEDN'T INVOLVE THE *POLICE* IN THIS, NEED WE?

NO, SIR. I HAVE THE SITUATION WELL IN HAND.

VERY WELL, THEN. TEND TO HIM.

YES, SIR. SLEEP WELL, SIR.

AND FOR GOODNESS' SAKE, AVA. DO GET SOME CLOTHES ON YOURSELF.

ROT IN HELL, DAMIEN.

HMPH!

SKRUKK
FOR A SECOND IT'S LIKE HE DOES RECOGNIZE ME, AFTER ALL. THEN HIS EYES GO COLD, A KILLER'S EYES.

AN ATOM BOMB GOES OFF BETWEEN MY LEGS.
WHUKK

KRAKK
A FREIGHT TRAIN BARRELS INTO MY JAW.
ANOTHER TRAIN.
SOMEWHERE FAR AWAY, AVA SCREAMS.

THE SOUNDS GO WET.

MAYBE HE KEEPS HITTING ME. I DON'T KNOW. I'M GONE.
GONE TO THAT PLACE WHERE THERE IS NO PAIN OR THOUGHT.

I WAKE UP IN MID-AIR. THE PAVEMENT RUSHES UP TO GIVE ME A BIG, SLOPPY KISS.

KHEFF

KHAGG

I FIND A PAY PHONE AND CALL AGAMEMNON AND ASK HIM TO COME AND PICK ME UP. HE MAKES ME PROMISE TO BUY HIM A TANK OF GAS AND A PIZZA WITH THE WORKS.
I GUESS I BLACK OUT AGAIN.
JESUS ON A STICK!
YOU AIN'T GONE BACK ON THE *SAUCE*, HAVE YOU, KID?
NO. I JUST GOT MUGGED.
ΚΟΠΡΟΣ ΦΑΝΕΤΑΙ

AGAMEMNON PULLS OVER AT A CHINESE JOINT AND SUCKS BACK SWEET-AND-SOUR ROADKILL WHILE I MOP THE BLOOD OFF MY FACE. THEN WE PICK UP THAT PIZZA I PROMISED HIM.
I WOULDA BET MY RIGHT NUT YOU BEEN HITTING THE BOTTLE AGAIN, SEEING YOU LIKE THAT... MAN, YOU WERE A *BAD* ONE BACK THEN.
I TELL YA, I COULD WRITE A BOOK...
ANOTHER STOP, THIS ONE FOR CHILI BURGERS. SOMEWHERE ALONG THE WAY I REALIZE I DON'T HAVE MY KEYS.
?!
I'LL HAVE TO PICK MY OWN LOCK.
THEN I SPOT MY MUSTANG, WHICH MAKES NO SENSE.
MY WORD, MR. McCARTHY. JUST LOOK AT YOU. YOU'RE NOT HAVING TROUBLE AGAIN, ARE YOU?
NO. I JUST GOT MUGGED.
WHY WOULD THEY RETURN MY CAR?
IT DOESN'T MAKE ANY SENSE.

MY DOOR'S NOT LOCKED.
THAT'S NOT MY COAT.

HER PURSE.
HER CIGARETTE SMOKE.

MY BEDROOM.

GET OUT OF HERE.

NO.
I MEAN IT. PUT YOUR CLOTHES BACK ON AND GET OUT OF HERE. NOW.
NO.
YOU HAD YOUR CHANCE. I WOULD HAVE STAYED AWAY. YOU NEVER WOULD HAVE SEEN ME AGAIN.
BUT YOU CAME FOR ME. YOU RISKED YOUR LIFE. YOU STILL CARE. YOU STILL WANT ME. AND I'M YOURS. NOW. TONIGHT.
YOU MAKE ME SICK. YOU AND THIS CRAZY GAME YOU'RE PLAYING. GET OUT OF MY LIFE ONCE AND FOR ALL OR I'LL BASH YOUR TEETH IN.

GO BACK TO YOUR MANSION. OR GO TO HELL. I DON'T CARE WHICH.
DO YOU WANT ME TO BEG? WOULD THAT AMUSE YOU? I'LL BEG. I'LL GROVEL. I HAVE NO SHAME. I'M NOTHING. I'M DIRT. I'M A LYING, TREACHEROUS WHORE WHO'S GOING TO GET WHAT I DESERVE.

BUT I MUST HAVE YOU FIRST. TONIGHT. NOW. TONIGHT, AND NEVER AGAIN. IF YOU CAN'T LOVE ME--HATE ME. IF YOU CAN'T FORGIVE ME --PUNISH ME.
OKAY.

KRAKKK

I CALL HER EVERY FOUL NAME THERE IS. SHE MAKES MY NAME SOUND LIKE MUSIC, LIKE A CHANT TO SOME DARK GOD.
SHE'S SLIPPERY WITH SWEAT.
BEFORE LONG MY HATRED'S SPENT BUT SHE WON'T LET GO. SHE KISSES AND COAXES ME AND THE FIRE GROWS AGAIN.

I'M DRAGGED TO THE GROUND BY A JUNGLE CAT. SHE DEVOURS ME AND I THANK HER FOR IT.

WE SOB AND SNIVEL AND BAWL OUT LOUD LIKE A COUPLE OF SNOT-NOSED KIDS.
WE MELT TOGETHER.
THE SHUDDER RUNS THROUGH BOTH OF US AS I SCREAM HER NAME.
AVA.
AVA!

I SAY ALL THE THINGS I SWORE I'D NEVER SAY AGAIN.
SHE OWNS ME.
BODY AND SOUL.

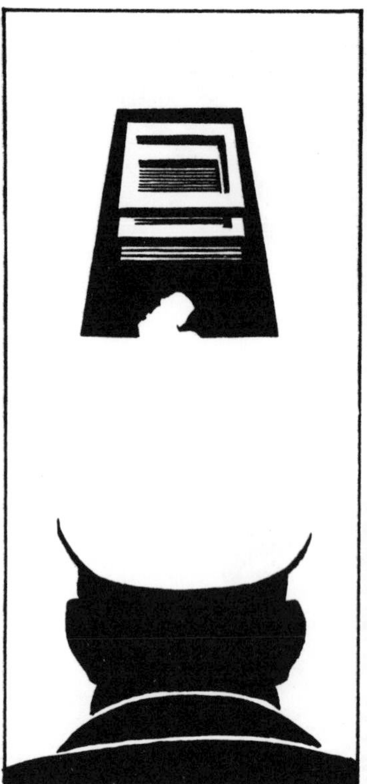

HER VOICE GOES FLAT, HOPELESS.

I THOUGHT TONIGHT WOULD MAKE IT EASIER. IT DOESN'T.
DAMIEN'S GOING TO GET HIS WISH, AFTER ALL. I'LL BEG HIM TO LET ME LIVE. BECAUSE OF YOU.
HE'S A MADMAN. A MADMAN. HE TORTURES ME. IT GIVES HIM PLEASURE. IT MAKES HIM FEEL POWER-FUL.
MANUTE --THE MAN WHO BEAT YOU-- HE'S A SPECIALIST AT INFLICTING PAIN. HIDEOUS PAIN, IN ALL THE PLACES YOU JUST GAVE ME JOY...
I THOUGHT I WAS READY TO DIE. I'M NOT.

...DAMIEN TALKS AND TALKS AND WATCHES WHILE MANUTE USES HIS NEEDLES--AND HIS FINGERS. THE FINGERS ARE THE WORST OF IT.
HE DOESN'T LEAVE A MARK ON ME. AT LEAST HE HASN'T SO FAR.
BUT IT'S WORSE EACH TIME. HE'S GETTING CLOSER TO HIS FINAL, SICK CLIMAX.
LATELY, DAMIEN'S SHOWN ME... *DEVICES* HE'S ACQUIRED. STRANGE, SHARP DEVICES FROM SPAIN AND CHINA AND AFRICA. HE SHOWS ME HOW THEY WORK.

HE SAYS I'LL BE VERY UGLY, BEFORE I DIE.
NO, AVA. *YOU* AREN'T GOING TO DIE. *YOU'RE* COMING WITH ME.

HER LAUGH IS BLACK AND BOTTOMLESS.
NO, DARLING. NO. HE'D FIND US. HE'D FIND US AND HE'D KILL YOU AND I COULDN'T STAND KNOWING I CAUSED THAT. HE *LETS* ME RUN AWAY! HE *LAUGHS* ABOUT IT! *HE KNOWS MANUTE WILL ALWAYS FIND ME!*
I'LL FIND A WAY! I SWEAR I WILL! HE'LL NEVER GET HIS HANDS ON YOU AGAIN!

KREEEK!

YOU HAVE BEEN VERY BAD, MRS. LORD. MR. LORD WILL REQUIRE THAT YOU BE DISCIPLINED. COME ALONG. I WILL FETCH YOUR COAT.

NO, DWIGHT. DON'T FIGHT HIM. HE'LL KILL YOU. HE'S NOT HUMAN. HE'LL KILL YOU.
YOU WOULD DO WELL TO LISTEN TO HER, SIR.

DWIGHT! NO! I BEG YOU, MY LOVE!
HE'LL KILL YOU!
FAPP
I PUNCH A VAULT DOOR.

FAPP
IT DOESN'T FALL DOWN, SO I PUNCH IT AGAIN.

WHUD
A WRECKING BALL HITS ME SQUARE IN THE CHEST.

HWUFF
COME ON, I'M READY FOR YOU, YOU SON OF A BITCH!!

KRASHH

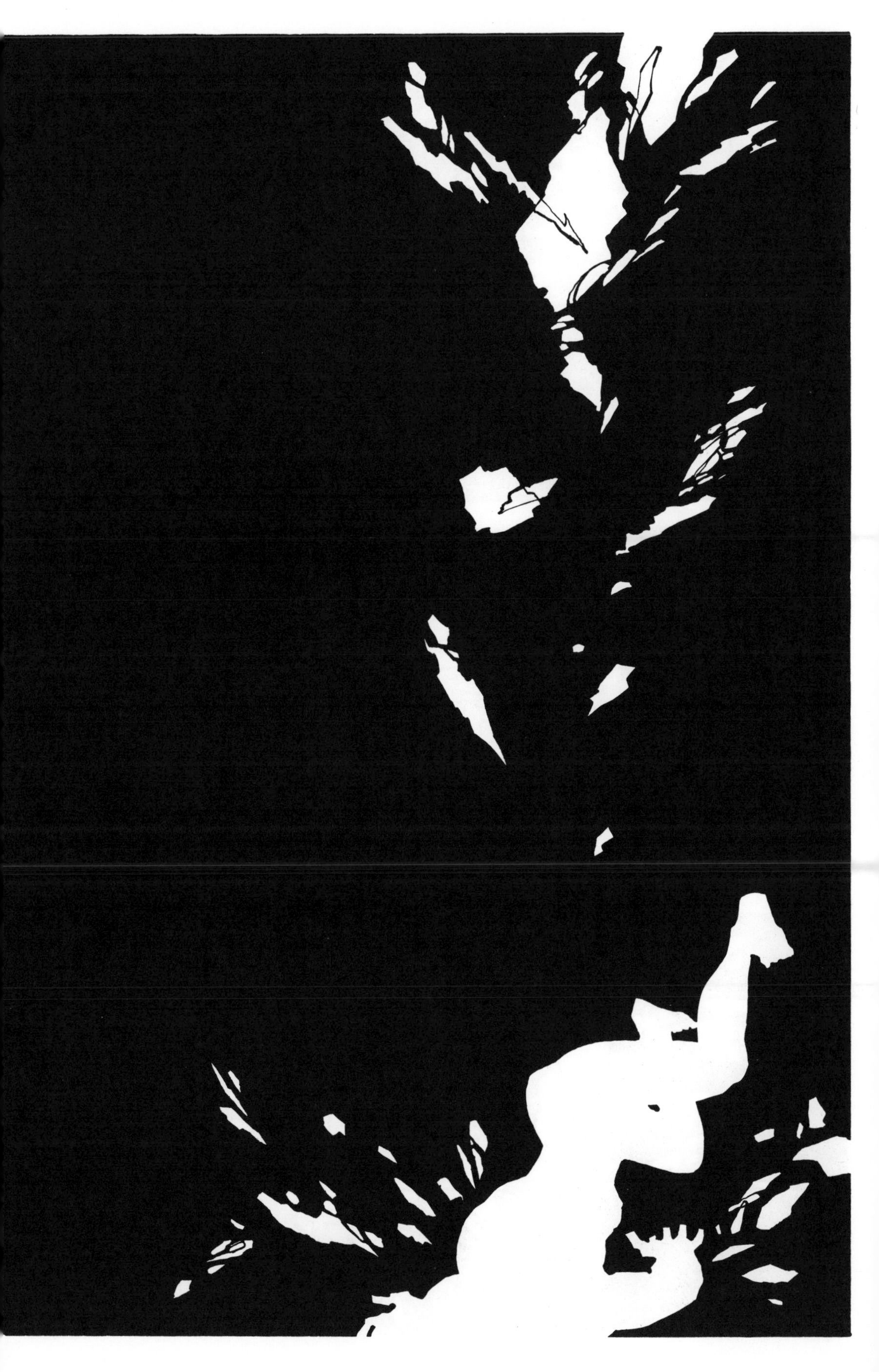

MRS. LORD.
YOUR COAT.

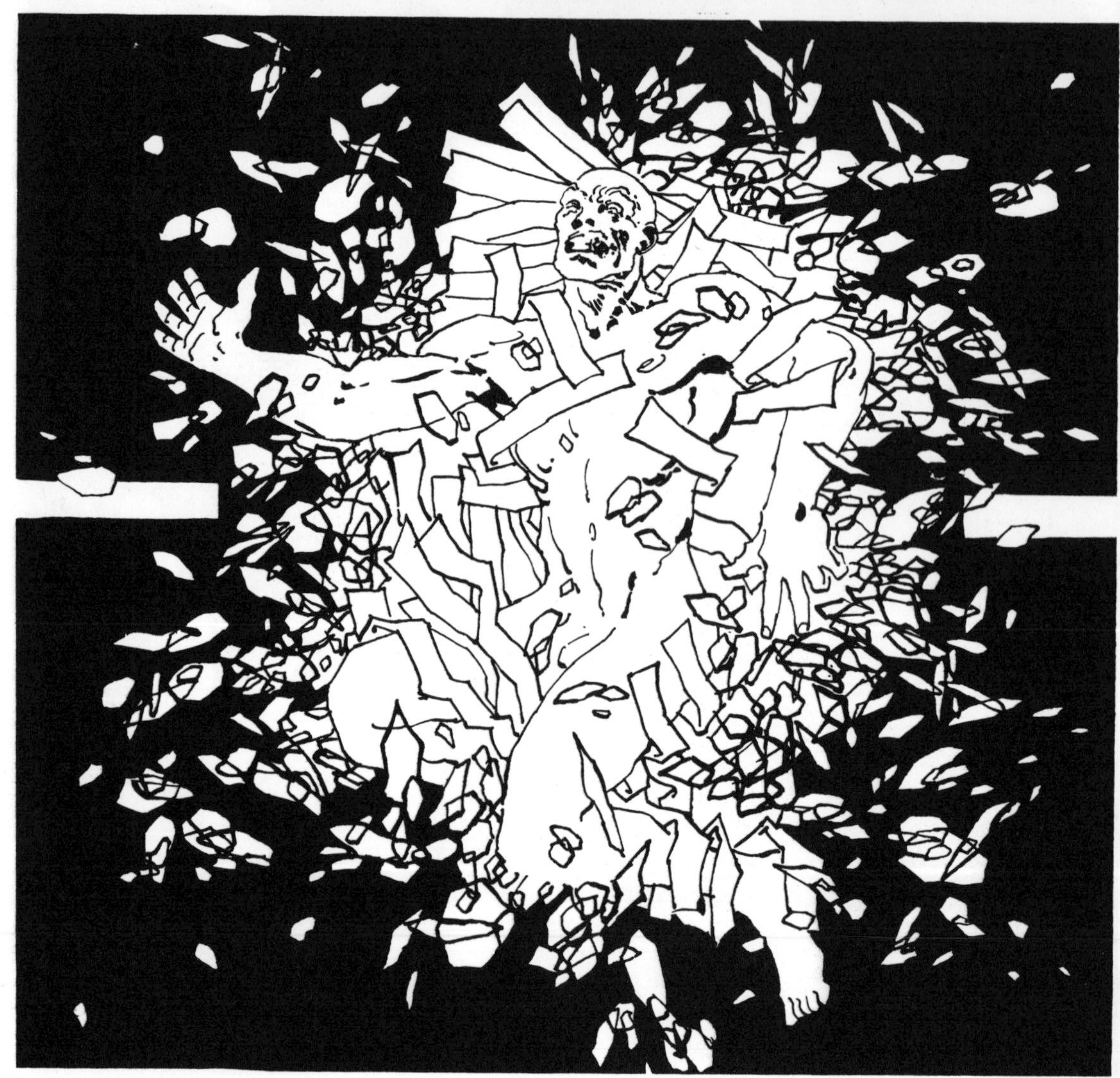

CHAPTER FOUR

AVA SCREAMS MY NAME.

I COME
AND GO.

NOTHING
MAKES ANY
SENSE.

AVA
SCREAMS
MY NAME.

I COME AND GO, RISING OUT OF IT, THEN SINKING AGAIN, DROWNING IN SOMETHING AS THICK AS PEA SOUP AND AS BLACK AS DEATH.
AVA SCREAMS MY NAME.
WITH AN OLD MAN'S ARMS I CLIMB MY WAY BACK UP.

HNH?

I SPIT OUT THE LAST OF THE PEA SOUP AND LET THE HEADLIGHTS CHASE AWAY THE BLACK SPOTS.
A LITTLE VOICE REMINDS ME THAT THERE'S A CAR BEHIND THE HEADLIGHTS.
WHUFF

KLUNK

KLUNK
HONK!

THE MONSTER IN MY GUT UNCURLS ITSELF AND ERUPTS FROM MY THROAT WITH AN ENDLESS, BLOODY ROAR.
THEY CAN'T TAKE HER AWAY FROM ME. NOT THIS TIME.

I KNOW EXACTLY WHAT TO DO.
I KNOW EXACTLY WHERE TO GO.
THIS TIME I DON'T FIGHT THE SMELLS--OR THE MEMORIES. I SUCK IT ALL IN LIKE IT WAS NECTAR, LETTING IT MAKE ME STRONG AND MEAN AND SURE.
A VOICE THAT'S MADE OUT OF WET GRAVEL BLARES OUT OF RATTY SPEAKERS, SINGING SOMETHING ABOUT BOURBON AND PATRIOTISM. IT'S SO LOUD I FEEL THE BEAT LIKE A PUNCH IN THE CHEST.
NANCY'S GOT THE CROWD WORKED UP TO A NEAR-DROOL.

SHE MAY BE SHOWING OFF EVERYTHING SHE'S GOT IN A JOINT FILLED WITH HORNY DRUNKS, BUT NANCY'S THE SAFEST GAL IN THE WORLD.

EVERYBODY KEEPS THEIR HANDS TO THEMSELVES. THEY KNOW WHAT HAPPENS TO YOU IF YOU DON'T.

I TRY TO BE PATIENT. I TRY NOT TO THINK ABOUT WHAT DAMIEN LORD IS DOING TO AVA, RIGHT NOW.

HOLD ON, BABY. JUST HOLD ON. I'M COMING FOR YOU. I'LL CARRY YOU OUT OF THAT MANSION IF I HAVE TO BURN THE PLACE TO THE GROUND.

BUT I CAN'T DO IT ALONE. I NEED SOMEBODY BIGGER AND MEANER THAN ME TO RUN INTERFERENCE -- AND TO TAKE MANUTE DOWN THE HARD WAY.

IT'S BEEN SIX MONTHS, DWIGHT. SIX MONTHS AND NOT SO MUCH AS A LOUSY PHONE CALL.
YEAH, I GUESS I'M A REAL JERK. SORRY.
I WASN'T EXPECTING FLOWERS OR ANYTHING, BUT A PHONE CALL WOULD'VE BEEN NICE. YOUR LOSS, WILDMAN.
SORRY. I'M A REAL JERK.
CUT OFF?!
IN THIS DIVE?!
I DON'T SEE YOU CUTTING OFF KING KONG OVER THERE!
HE DON'T EVER GET CUT OFF. AND WATCH WHAT YOU CALL HIM.
IT'S OKAY, JOSIE. HE'S FROM OUT OF TOWN. HE DOESN'T KNOW NOTHING.
TELL HER, MAN!
WE'LL BACK YOU UP!
TOURISTS. THIS COULD GET UGLY.

BUDDY, MAYBE YOU OUGHT TO TAKE SOME FRIENDLY ADVICE AND HAUL ON OUT OF HERE. YOU'VE HAD A FEW TOO MANY. WE ALL KNOW WHAT THAT'S LIKE. BUT YOU'RE HEADED FOR TROUBLE, MOUTHING OFF LIKE YOU BEEN. GO GET YOURSELF SOME SLEEP.
WE'LL BACK YOU UP!
TELL HIM OFF!
I'M NOT TAKING ANY ORDERS FROM YOU--OR FROM THAT COW, EITHER, BIG GUY!
MARV'S IN ALTOGETHER TOO GENEROUS A MOOD TONIGHT.
I'LL HAVE TO DO SOMETHING ABOUT THAT.
YOU SHOULDN'T OUGHT TO USE LANGUAGE LIKE THAT. NOT WHEN IT'S A LADY YOU'RE TALKING ABOUT.
"LADY"? I DON'T KNOW. SHE LOOKS MORE LIKE A COW TO ME!

THERE'S NO CALL FOR GETTING NASTY.

IT'S OKAY, MARV. STAY OUT OF THIS ONE.

SHE SMELLS LIKE A COW, TOO! BUT MAYBE THAT TURNS A GUY LIKE YOU ON! IF I LOOKED LIKE YOU, I'D SETTLE FOR A COW!

YOU ARE REALLY PUSHING IT.

HELL, I BET COWS ARE GREAT! YOU GET ALL THOSE EXTRA HOOTERS TO PLAY WITH!

YOU BETTER SHUT YOUR TRAP AND GET LOST.

SHOW HIM, MAN! SHOW HIM!
I GOT SOMETHING THAT MAKES ME A BIGGER GUY THAN YOU, UGLY!
NOW THAT THERE IS ONE DAMN BIG GUN.
COOL SPEED RIG, TOO. MUST'VE SET YOU BACK A BUNDLE.
I GOT TO TELL YOU, I'M IMPRESSED. I REALLY AM.

HE'S BEGGING FOR IT, MAN! BLOW HIM AWAY!
WE'LL BACK YOU UP!
I WILL! I'LL DO IT! I'LL BLOW YOUR DAMN HEAD OFF!
NOW SET 'EM UP, COW!
OKAY. ANOTHER ROUND. ON THE HOUSE. IT'S OKAY, MARV. NO TROUBLE.
YEAH, WE ALL HAVE A FEW TOO MANY SOMETIMES.
IT JUST GETS MY GOAT WHEN GUYS TALK ABOUT DAMES THAT WAY.

MOOOOoo
YOU'RE REALLY STARTING TO HONK ME OFF.

MoooOOOOoooo
KRAKK!
KRUNCH!

BUNCH OF PANSIES...
♪
I COULD USE SOME SLEEP.
OWE THE WIFE A CALL.
GET A GOOD START IN THE MORN-ING.
MARV-- I NEED YOUR HELP.
DWIGHT! I DIDN'T EVEN SEE YOU THERE, BUDDY!
WHAT CAN I DO YOU FOR?

IT'S BAD, MARV. IT MEANS GOING UP AGAINST A LOT OF GUNS.
COUNT ME IN. BOY, THAT NANCY SURE IS SOMETHING...
EVERYBODY KEEPS THEIR HANDS TO THEMSELVES. THEY'VE SEEN WHAT HAPPENS TO YOU IF YOU DON'T.
NANCY'S GOT A GUARDIAN ANGEL.
SEVEN-FEET-PLUS OF MUSCLE AND MAYHEM THAT GOES BY THE NAME OF MARV.

MOST PEOPLE THINK MARV IS CRAZY, BUT I DON'T BELIEVE THAT.

I'M NO SHRINK AND I'M NOT SAYING I'VE GOT MARV ALL FIGURED OUT OR ANYTHING, BUT "CRAZY" JUST DOESN'T EXPLAIN HIM. NOT TO ME. SOMETIMES I THINK HE'S RETARDED, A BIG, BRUTAL KID WHO NEVER LEARNED THE GROUND RULES ABOUT HOW PEOPLE ARE SUPPOSED TO ACT AROUND EACH OTHER. BUT THAT DOESN'T HAVE THE RIGHT RING TO IT EITHER. NO, IT'S MORE LIKE THERE'S NOTHING WRONG WITH MARV, NOTHING AT ALL--EXCEPT THAT HE HAD THE ROTTEN LUCK OF BEING BORN AT THE WRONG TIME IN HISTORY. HE'D HAVE BEEN OKAY IF HE'D BEEN BORN A COUPLE OF THOUSAND YEARS AGO. HE'D BE RIGHT AT HOME ON SOME ANCIENT BATTLEFIELD, SWINGING AN AX INTO SOMEBODY'S FACE. OR IN A ROMAN ARENA, TAKING A SWORD TO OTHER GLADIATORS LIKE HIM.

THEY'D HAVE TOSSED HIM GIRLS LIKE NANCY, BACK THEN.

AND NOW ALL HE CAN DO IS WATCH.

SO WE WATCH NANCY AND WE FINISH OFF THE BOTTLE, LETTING ITS LIQUID DARKNESS FILL US BOTH. WHEN I'M SURE HE'S HAD ENOUGH TO MAKE HIM GOOD AND DANGEROUS I TELL HIM ABOUT AVA AND HIS EYES GO KILLER RED. I KNOW HE'S WILLING TO DIE FOR ME, IF THAT'S WHAT IT TAKES.

THE POOR SLOB. I'M USING HIM.

SO I'M USING HIM. SO WHAT? SO HE BREAKS THE FACES I WANT HIM TO BREAK INSTEAD OF SOMEBODY ELSE'S. SO HE HELPS ME GET AVA BACK IN MY ARMS INSTEAD OF SLEEPING IT OFF IN A FLOP-HOUSE OR A GUTTER OR A DRUNK TANK.

HIS LIFE ISN'T WORTH A DAMN ANYWAY. IF I DON'T GET HIM KILLED, THE WORLD WILL, ONE WAY OR ANOTHER. IT HAS TO KILL HIM. IT'S GOT NO PLACE FOR HIM.

THE POOR SLOB.

I HATE MYSELF.

CHAPTER FIVE

I'VE NEVER SEEN MARV WITH A GUN BEFORE. THE WAY HE PLAYS WITH IT IS REALLY DISTURBING.
I FINALLY REALIZE HOW BEAT UP I AM. SOMEBODY'S TAKEN A POWER SANDER TO THE SKIN OF MY BACK AND WORKED MY KIDNEYS OVER WITH A JACK-HAMMER. MY SPINE IS A TANGLED CHAIN. A BIG, WET BRUISE SQUATS ON MY SKULL WHERE MY FACE OUGHT TO BE. MY TONGUE MOVES ALL ON ITS OWN, PROBING A SORE SPOT TILL A MOLAR COMES LOOSE. I SPIT IT OUT WITH A CHUCKLE AND MARV SHOOTS ME A LOOK, THEN GIVES WITH A CROOKED SMILE, LIKE HE KNOWS HOW I FEEL.
I MEAN IT, MARV. I WANT YOU TO LEAVE THAT THING IN THE CAR. NOBODY'S GOING TO GET KILLED TONIGHT.
AW, DWIGHT. YOU'RE NO FUN AT ALL.
HE'S WRONG ABOUT THAT.
I'M NOT LIKE HIM.

WE SPLIT UP AT THE GATE.

IT DOESN'T TAKE MARV LONG TO GET THEIR ATTENTION.
CRASH!
GRAAA

...YOU!
YOU'RE THE BUM WHO HURT MY PAL!
BREKKT

CRASH
WHUDD
WHUDD
WHUDD
WHUDD
WHUDD
WHUDD
WHUDD

HEFF HEFF HEFF

KHOFF

WHUDD
WHUDD
WHUDD
WHUDD
WHUDD
WHUDD
WHUDD

DAMIEN LORD.
AVA'S HUSBAND.

WHERE IS SHE? WHERE'S AVA?
WHAT HAVE YOU DONE WITH HER?
I HAVEN'T THE SLIGHTEST NOTION OF WHAT SORT OF NONSENSE MY WIFE HAS FILLED YOUR HEAD WITH, STRANGER -- NOR DO I CARE.

THE WOMAN IS UTTERLY PATH-OLOGICAL...
GET AWAY FROM THAT DESK.
I'M WARNING YOU, MAN. DON'T GIVE ME AN EXCUSE.

BLAM!
THOK!

KRAK!
KRAK!

KRAK

OH, JESUS. OH, JESUS.

I KILLED HIM. OH, JESUS.
YOU SURE DID.

I KNEW I COULD COUNT ON YOU. SEX ALWAYS MADE YOU STUPID. READY TO BELIEVE ANYTHING.
AND THAT TEMPER OF YOURS. YOU NEVER COULD CONTROL IT. YOU'VE MURDERED AN INNOCENT MAN, DARLING. AND YOU'VE MADE ME A VERY RICH WOMAN.

THANKS, SUCKER!
BLAM!

AVA.
NO.
BLAM!

I'M AFRAID I'M NOT A TERRIBLY GOOD SHOT. THIS MIGHT TAKE A WHILE. IT'D BE SO MUCH SIMPLER IF MANUTE WERE HERE TO KILL YOU, LIKE HE'S SUPPOSED TO BE. GOODNESS KNOWS WHAT'S KEEPING HIM. SWEETHEART-- DO US BOTH A FAVOR AND STAY STILL LONG ENOUGH FOR ME TO BLOW YOUR BRAINS OUT.
AVA. YOU CAN'T BE DOING THIS.

I CAN DO WHATEVER I WANT, YOU SCHMUCK! I'M IN CHARGE HERE!
"I'M IN CHARGE" --GOD, I'VE WAITED YEARS TO SAY THAT. YEARS. NIGHT AFTER NIGHT, FLAT ON MY BACK, MAKING ALL THE RIGHT NOISES WHILE DAMIEN DID WHAT YOU MEN DO. I WAITED. I PLANNED. FOR THE MOMENT I COULD HAVE IT ALL. I KNEW IT WOULD WORK! I KNEW IT!
HUK
HUKK
BLAGGG

SORRY TO BE SUCH A CHATTER-BOX. I CAN'T HELP MYSELF. THIS IS SUCH A RARE OPPORTUNITY. I ALMOST NEVER GET THE CHANCE TO STOP ACTING --TO STOP *LYING*. TO LET SOMEBODY SEE THE REAL ME. MAYBE IT'S FOR THE BEST THAT MANUTE DIDN'T SHOW UP, AFTER ALL. IT'S ONLY RIGHT THAT I GET TO SHARE THIS MOMENT WITH YOU.
YOU'RE *INSANE!*

INSANE? HA! THAT'S SO *EASY*, SO *CONVENIENT*--AND SO *WRONG*. *CRAZY* PEOPLE PUSH *SHOPPING CARTS* DOWN THE STREETS AND TALK *NONSENSE*. *CRAZY* PEOPLE SIT IN *PADDED CELLS* AND SOIL THEIR *PANTS*. A *MADWOMAN* COULDN'T HAVE PULLED THIS OFF.
NO. THERE'S A WORD FOR WHAT I AM, BUT NOBODY USES IT ANY-MORE. NOBODY WANTS TO SEE THE SIMPLE TRUTH. IF THEY DID, THEY'D KILL PEOPLE LIKE ME AS SOON AS WE REVEALED OURSELVES.

BUT THEY DON'T. THEY CLOSE THEIR EYES AND BLATHER ABOUT *PSYCHOLOGY* AND SAY *NOBODY* IS TRULY *EVIL*. THAT'S WHY I'VE *WON*. THAT'S WHY I *ALWAYS* WIN.

BLAM!
THANKS FOR LISTENING TO ALL THAT, HONEY.

BLAM!
?

BLAM!

KASHHH

THUMP
THUMP
THUMP
THUMP

THUD
BLAM!
BLAM!
SPAK

CLICK
CLICK
CLICK

DAMN!

HMM...
OH, OFFICER... I WAS SO TERRIFIED... THERE WAS BLOOD EVERY-WHERE!... "BLOOD EVERYWHERE" ...THAT'S GOOD...

IS THIS THE POLICE? OH, GOD! IT'S HORRIBLE! COME QUICKLY! IT'S HORRIBLE! THERE'S BLOOD EVERY-WHERE! I THINK HE'S DEAD!
MY HUSBAND! HE'S NOT MOVING! I HEARD GUNSHOTS! AND DWIGHT WAS BEATING HIM! HE WOULDN'T STOP! THERE'S BLOOD EVERYWHERE!

I'M SORRY! I'LL TRY TO MAKE SENSE! I'M AVA LORD! IT'S MY HUSBAND! DAMIEN! THAT'S RIGHT! DAMIEN LORD!
YES! I SAW HIM! IT WAS DWIGHT! DWIGHT McCARTHY! HE'S CRAZY! CRAZY! HE'S BEEN MAKING THREATS! AND NOW THERE'S BLOOD EVERYWHERE! PLEASE HURRY!

TIK!
THE RICHEST WOMAN IN SIN CITY...

HAHAHA HA HA HA HA HA HA HA HA HA HA HA HA

HONK
I HANDLED THAT BIG GUY JUST LIKE I PROMISED, DWIGHT.
LUNATIC!

I DIDN'T KILL HIM. HELL, I DIDN'T EVEN CRIPPLE HIM. SIX MONTHS IN TRACTION, TOPS. I TOOK AN EYE OUT OF HIM, THOUGH.
AND BEFORE YOU SAY ANYTHING, I KNOW I WAS SUPPOSED TO USE YOUR MUSTANG FOR THE GETAWAY. BUT THEN I SAW THIS BEAUTY SITTING THERE, KEYS IN THE IGNITION AND EVERYTHING. I COULDN'T PASS UP A CHANCE TO TAKE A SPIN IN AN HONEST-TO-GOD TUCKER!

YOU KNOW THEY ONLY MADE A COUPLE DOZEN OF THESE BABIES? I SAW A MOVIE ABOUT IT ONCE. ANY-WAYS, I'M REAL SORRY ABOUT YOUR MUSTANG AND I'LL GO BACK FOR IT ONCE WE GOT YOU PATCHED UP.

NEVER MIND ABOUT MY CAR, MARV. JUST GET ME TO OLD TOWN. I GOT FRIENDS THERE. AND COULD YOU TURN THAT RADIO DOWN?
I'M QUAKING COLD FROM HEAD TO TOE. ALL MY WARMTH SQUIRTS OUT OF ME, KEEPING PERFECT TIME WITH MY HEARTBEAT. ONE OF MY LUNGS SUCKS AIR THROUGH A HOLE IN MY CHEST EVERY TIME I LOOSEN MY GRIP ON IT.
I DON'T THINK I'VE EVER BEEN SHOT UP AS BAD AS THIS BEFORE.
YOU *KIDDING?* THAT'S *MERLE! MERLE HAGGARD!* THE GREATEST COUNTRY SINGER THERE EVER *WAS!*
I'M A JERK AND AN IDIOT AND A MURDERER ON MY WAY TO BECOMING A CORPSE, AND MARV IS TALKING ABOUT MERLE HAGGARD.

...I THOUGHT OLD MERLE HAD LOST IT, FOR A FEW YEARS THERE. GONE ALL *SQUISHY,* SINGING CRAP LIKE *"YOU PUT ME ON A NATURAL HIGH."* I COULDN'T *BELIEVE* IT WHEN HE SANG THAT ONE.
I MEAN, WHAT'S NEXT, MERLE? *"YOU LIGHT UP MY LIFE"?* CHRIST...

KLUMP
!
...BUT THIS *NEW* TUNE...

EEEEE
...THIS *"ME AND CRIPPLED SOLDIERS,"* THIS IS AS GOOD AS HE *EVER* WAS. JUST SHOWS TO GO YOU. YOU NEVER CAN TELL.
SORRY...
POLI

EEE
PULL OVER!
...HERE I AM JABBERING, WITH *YOU* LEAKING ALL OVER THE PLACE. YOU'RE DAMN LUCKY ALL THAT DAME HAD WAS A .32 ...

OOF!
...WE WOULDN'T EVEN BE HAVING THIS CONVERSATION IF SHE'D USED A REAL GUN ON YOU. EVEN SO, GETTING SHOT IN THE FACE ISN'T HIGH ON MY LIST OF HOW TO HAVE A GOOD TIME.
JUST HOLD ON. I'LL GET YOU TO A GUY I KNOW.

YAAAA
KLINK
HE'S GOOD WITH BULLETS AND HE DON'T ASK QUESTIONS.

NO. OLD TOWN. TAKE ME TO OLD TOWN.
LET ME LEVEL WITH YOU, PAL. I KNOW SOMETHING ABOUT THESE THINGS AND YOU AIN'T GOING TO MAKE IT TO OLD TOWN. THAT'S A GOOD TWENTY MINUTES AWAY AND YOU'RE ABOUT TEN MINUTES FROM BEING DEAD.

I'LL MAKE IT. I WON'T DIE. I'VE GOT TOO MUCH I HAVE TO DO TO LET MYSELF DIE.

CHAPTER SIX

YOU DON'T KNOW WHAT HE'S CAPABLE OF! THE THINGS HE SAID! EVEN WHILE HE WAS BEATING THE LIFE OUT OF POOR, DEAR DAMIEN--HE KEPT TELLING ME WHAT HE WAS GOING TO DO TO ME!
I DON'T KNOW WHERE I FOUND THE COURAGE TO GRAB THE GUN--I FIRED AND FIRED--BUT HE LAUGHED! HE JUST KEPT LAUGHING!

HE LEFT A LOT OF BLOOD, MRS. LORD. HE WON'T GET FAR.
I KNOW IT'S DIFFICULT, BUT PLEASE TRY TO STAY CALM. YOU SAID YOU KNEW HIM...
I'M SORRY, LIEUTENANT. YOU'VE BEEN SO VERY PATIENT WITH ME. HERE WE'VE BARELY MET, BUT ALREADY I FEEL I CAN TRUST YOU.
THE KILLER'S NAME IS DWIGHT McCARTHY. WE WERE... TOGETHER, FOR A TIME, A FEW YEARS AGO...

...HE STARTED IMAGINING THINGS. FOLLOWING ME, WHEREVER I WENT.
THERE WAS A CAT I HAD. A BURMESE NAMED MUFFIN. I LOVED THAT CAT. BUT TO DWIGHT SHE WAS JUST ANOTHER THING TO BE JEALOUS ABOUT. ANOTHER THREAT. HE CUT HER EYES OUT. HE SAID HE'D DO THE SAME THING TO ME.

I RAN AWAY. I MET DAMIEN. I THOUGHT I WAS SAFE. BUT THEN HE STARTED CALLING. LATE AT NIGHT. ALWAYS AT NIGHT. AND NOW--NOW DAMIEN'S DEAD AND...OH, PLEASE, LIEUTENANT. HOLD ME. HOLD ME TIGHT. JUST FOR A MOMENT...

NOTHING LIKE A WIDOW IN NEED OF COMFORT. I GOT A STIFFY JUST WATCHING. IF YOU'RE NOT A COMPLETE DOPE, YOU'LL BE CHECKING BACK ON THAT ONE.
I'M A MARRIED MAN, BOB.

NO DISRESPECT TO THE LITTLE WOMAN, MORT, BUT YOU DON'T PASS UP A CHANCE LIKE THAT! WHAT'S THE POINT OF BEING A SIN CITY COP IF YOU DON'T GET ANY USE OUT OF THE PERKS?
THAT'S ENOUGH, BOB. YOU SHUT THE HELL UP.

WE'RE CUTTING THROUGH LITTLE SAIGON WHEN A POLICE CHOPPER SPOTS US. MARV HOLDS A CLINIC ON EVASIVE DRIVING AND CASUAL PROPERTY DAMAGE. I HOLD MY GUTS IN AND DO MY BEST TO STAY CONSCIOUS. THINKING ABOUT AVA HELPS.

AVA.

YOU GOT ME GOOD, BABE. JUST WHEN I WAS PULLING IT BACK TOGETHER YOU COME ALONG AND RIP MY HEART OUT ONE MORE TIME. ONLY THIS TIME YOU CROSSED A FINAL, FATAL LINE. YOU TRICKED ME INTO DOING SOMETHING THERE'S NO COMING BACK FROM. YOU'VE DAMNED MY SOUL TO HELL.

THEN THE MAYBES KICK IN. MAYBE I SHOULDN'T PUT THE BLAME ON YOU. MAYBE ONCE I LET THE MONSTER OUT SOMETHING BAD WAS SURE TO HAPPEN, JUST LIKE IT ALWAYS HAS. MAYBE A KILLER'S A KILLER AND I WAS JUST BORN THAT WAY. MAYBE ALL YOU DID WAS GIVE ME A TARGET.

MAYBE. BUT I'M GOING TO GO AHEAD AND BLAME YOU ANYWAY. I HAVE TO BLAME YOU. HATE'S THE ONLY THING KEEPING ME GOING, SO I'M HOLDING ON TO IT.

I CAN'T SEEM TO GET ANY AIR IN. I'M GULPING A LOT. IT SOUNDS AWFUL.

PAVEMENT GIVES WAY TO COBBLE-STONE. THE CITY'S NOISE RECEDES. WE'RE IN A QUIET NEIGHBORHOOD, WHERE ALL THE SOUNDS OF PASSION AND VIOLENCE ARE LOCKED AWAY BEHIND CLOSED DOORS.
OLD TOWN.
IT'S HARDER THAN EVER TO BREATHE. I CAN'T SLOW MY HEART DOWN. THIS DOESN'T LOOK GOOD.
ONE SQUAD CAR STILL CHASES US. MUST BE A ROOKIE DRIVING. OTHER-WISE HE WOULD'VE KNOWN TO BACK OFF. THE POOR BASTARD...

HELLBOY

BLAM

BLAM!
BLAM!
BLAM!

BRAKABRAKABRAK

...THE POOR, DUMB ROOKIE. HIS BUDDIES SHOULD HAVE TOLD HIM THAT THE GIRLS OF OLD TOWN HAVE LAWS ALL THEIR OWN--
--AND THEY DON'T TAKE KINDLY TO COPS.

HAW!
THIS IS GREAT!
YOU'RE A GENIUS, KID!

BRAKABRAKA BUDDABLAM
BLAM BLAM BUDDABLAM
BRAKA BLAM
BLAM

POOM!
POOM!

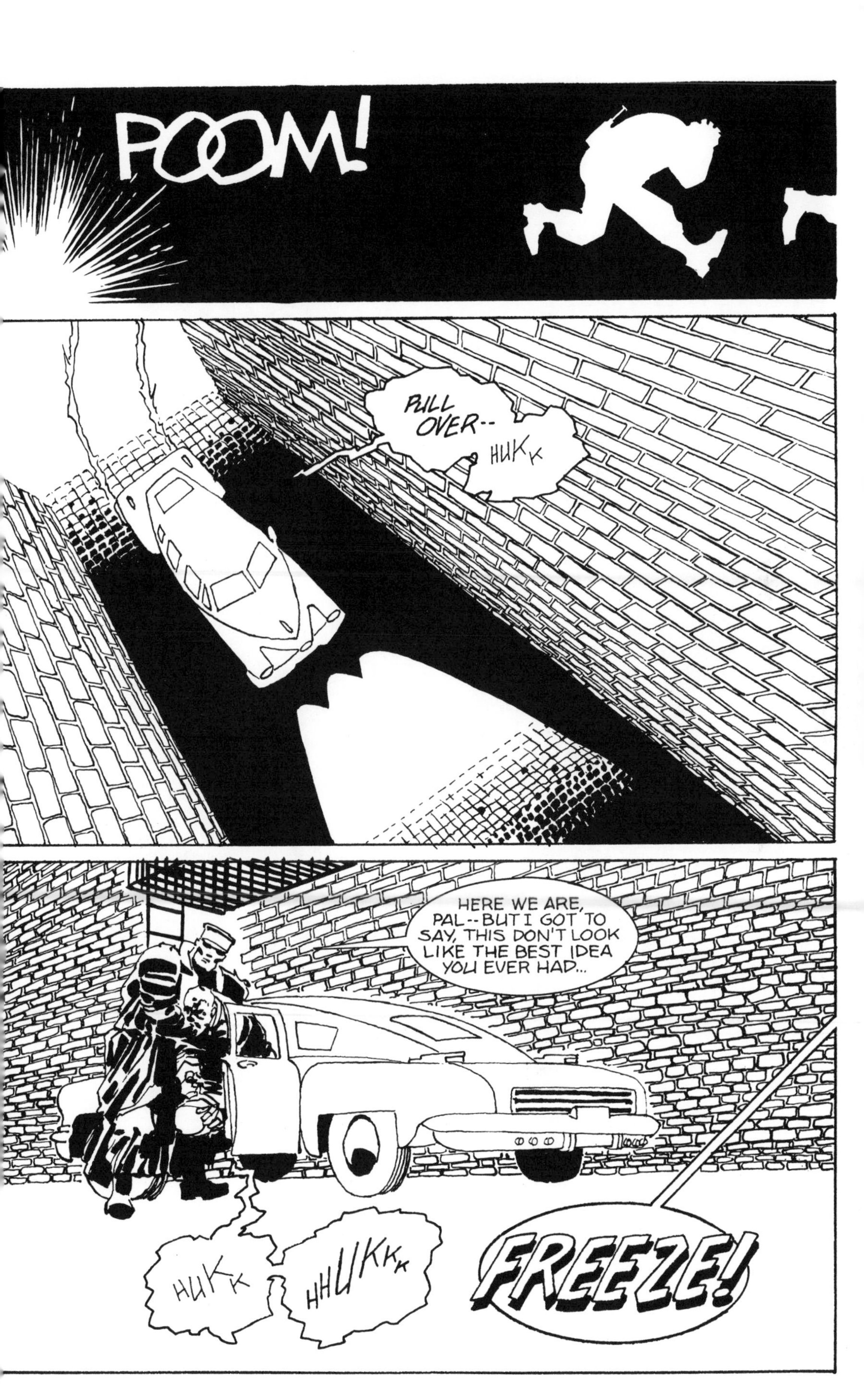
POOM!
PULL OVER-- HUKK
HERE WE ARE, PAL--BUT I GOT TO SAY, THIS DON'T LOOK LIKE THE BEST IDEA YOU EVER HAD...
HUKK
HHUKKK
FREEZE!

YOU BOYS HAVE TEN SECONDS TO TELL US WHAT YOU'RE DOING BRINGING COPS TO OLD TOWN. THEN THINGS GET NASTY.

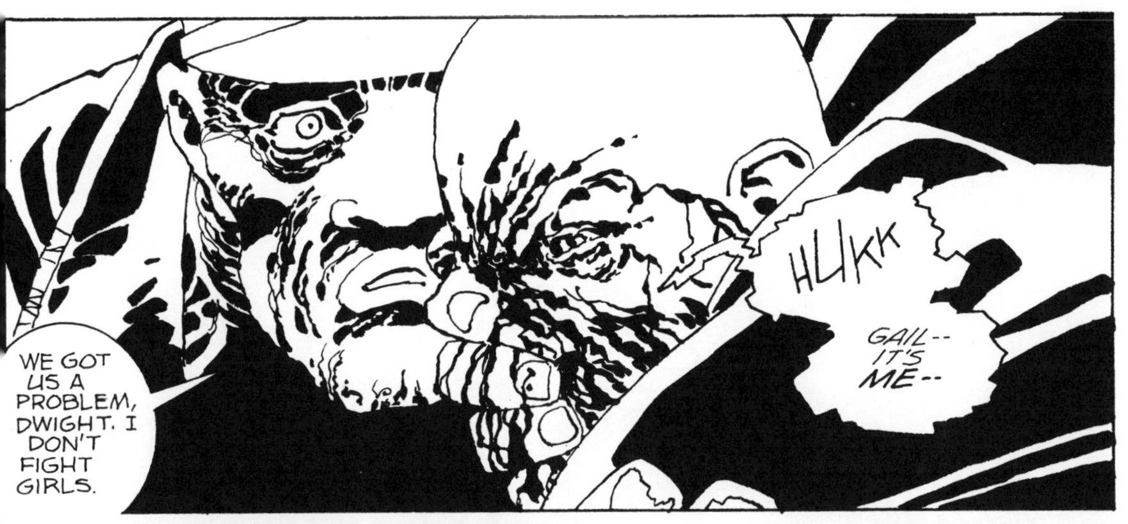
HUKK
GAIL-- IT'S ME--
WE GOT US A PROBLEM, DWIGHT. I DON'T FIGHT GIRLS.

DWIGHT.

OH, BABY. WHAT HAVE THEY DONE TO YOU?
HUKKK

A CORKSCREW STABS ME SQUARE IN THE CHEST -- AND *TWISTS.*

IT'S HIS HEART! GET MOLLY!

BRIING!
IT'S ABOUT TIME...

LIEUTENANT. YOU'RE SO KIND TO CALL.
...NO, I WASN'T SLEEPING. I HAVEN'T SLEPT AT *ALL*. NOT FOR *TWO DAYS*. I'M JUST *FRANTIC*. I'M *JUMPING* AT EVERY *SOUND*--JUST *KNOWING* HE'S STILL *OUT* THERE. I GUESS I'M NOT A VERY STRONG PERSON.
YOU SHOULDN'T BE SO HARD ON YOURSELF, MRS. LORD.
YOU'RE HAVING A VERY UNDERSTANDABLE REACTION. PLEASE, IF THERE'S ANYTHING AT ALL I CAN DO FOR YOU...
I HATE MYSELF FOR SAYING THIS, BUT--NO. NO, I COULDN'T ASK...
...WELL... OH, GOD, I'M SO *WEAK*...
...IT'S JUST THAT I DON'T KNOW IF I COULD BEAR TO BE ALONE TONIGHT...

CHAPTER SEVEN

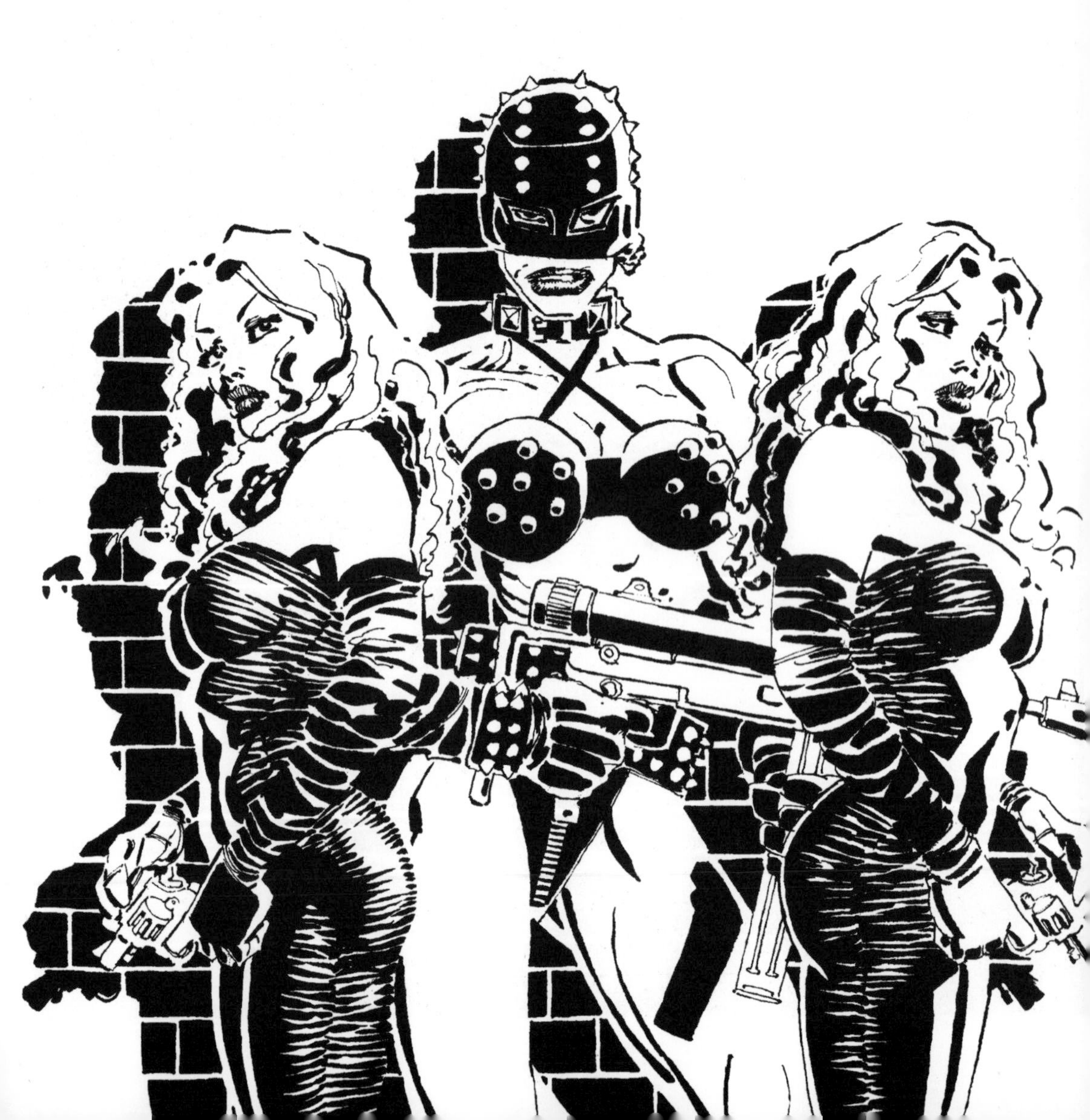

MY
HEART
BEATS.

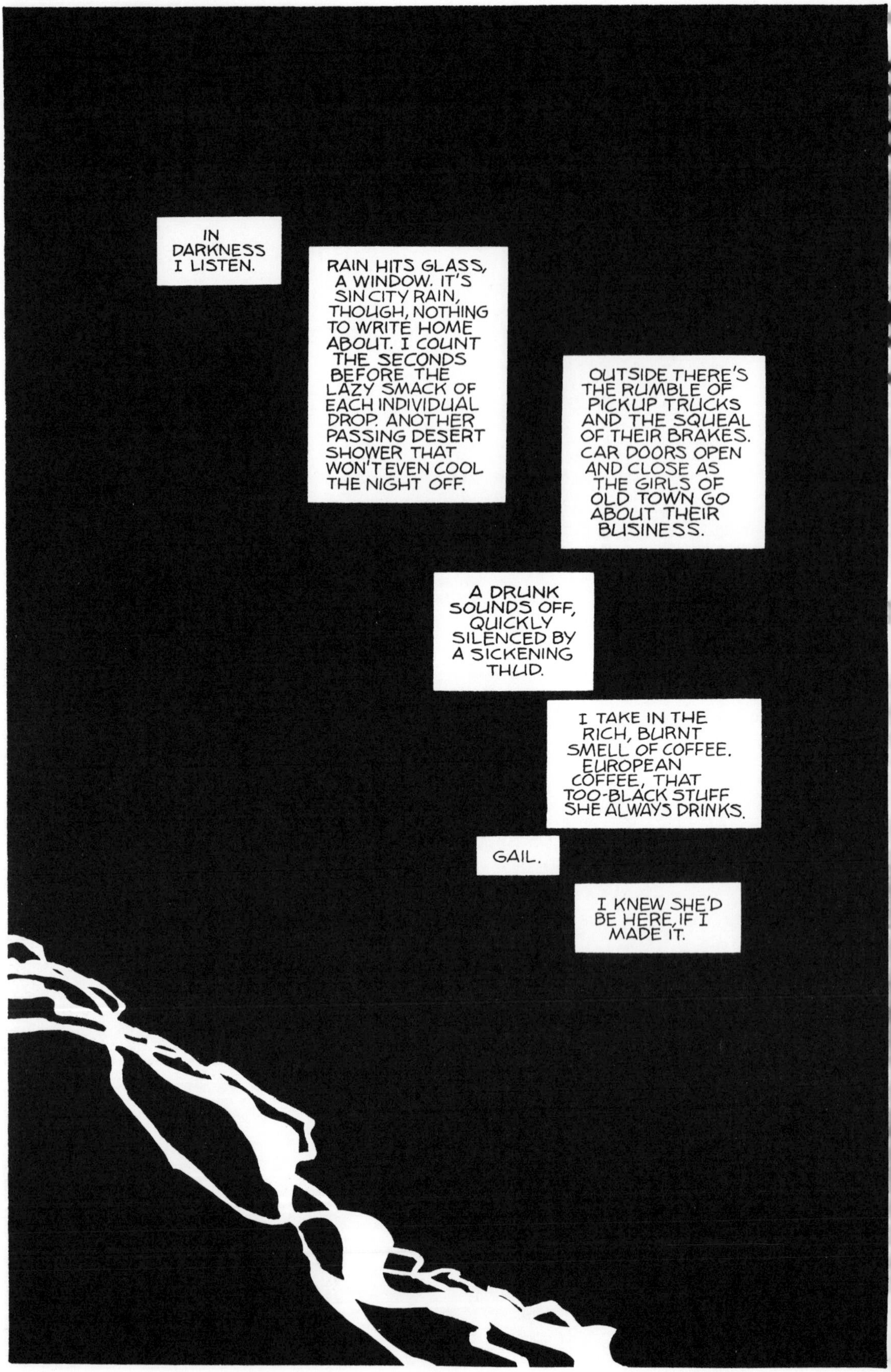

IN DARKNESS I LISTEN.
RAIN HITS GLASS, A WINDOW. IT'S SIN CITY RAIN, THOUGH, NOTHING TO WRITE HOME ABOUT. I COUNT THE SECONDS BEFORE THE LAZY SMACK OF EACH INDIVIDUAL DROP. ANOTHER PASSING DESERT SHOWER THAT WON'T EVEN COOL THE NIGHT OFF.
OUTSIDE THERE'S THE RUMBLE OF PICKUP TRUCKS AND THE SQUEAL OF THEIR BRAKES. CAR DOORS OPEN AND CLOSE AS THE GIRLS OF OLD TOWN GO ABOUT THEIR BUSINESS.
A DRUNK SOUNDS OFF, QUICKLY SILENCED BY A SICKENING THUD.
I TAKE IN THE RICH, BURNT SMELL OF COFFEE. EUROPEAN COFFEE, THAT TOO-BLACK STUFF SHE ALWAYS DRINKS.
GAIL.
I KNEW SHE'D BE HERE, IF I MADE IT.

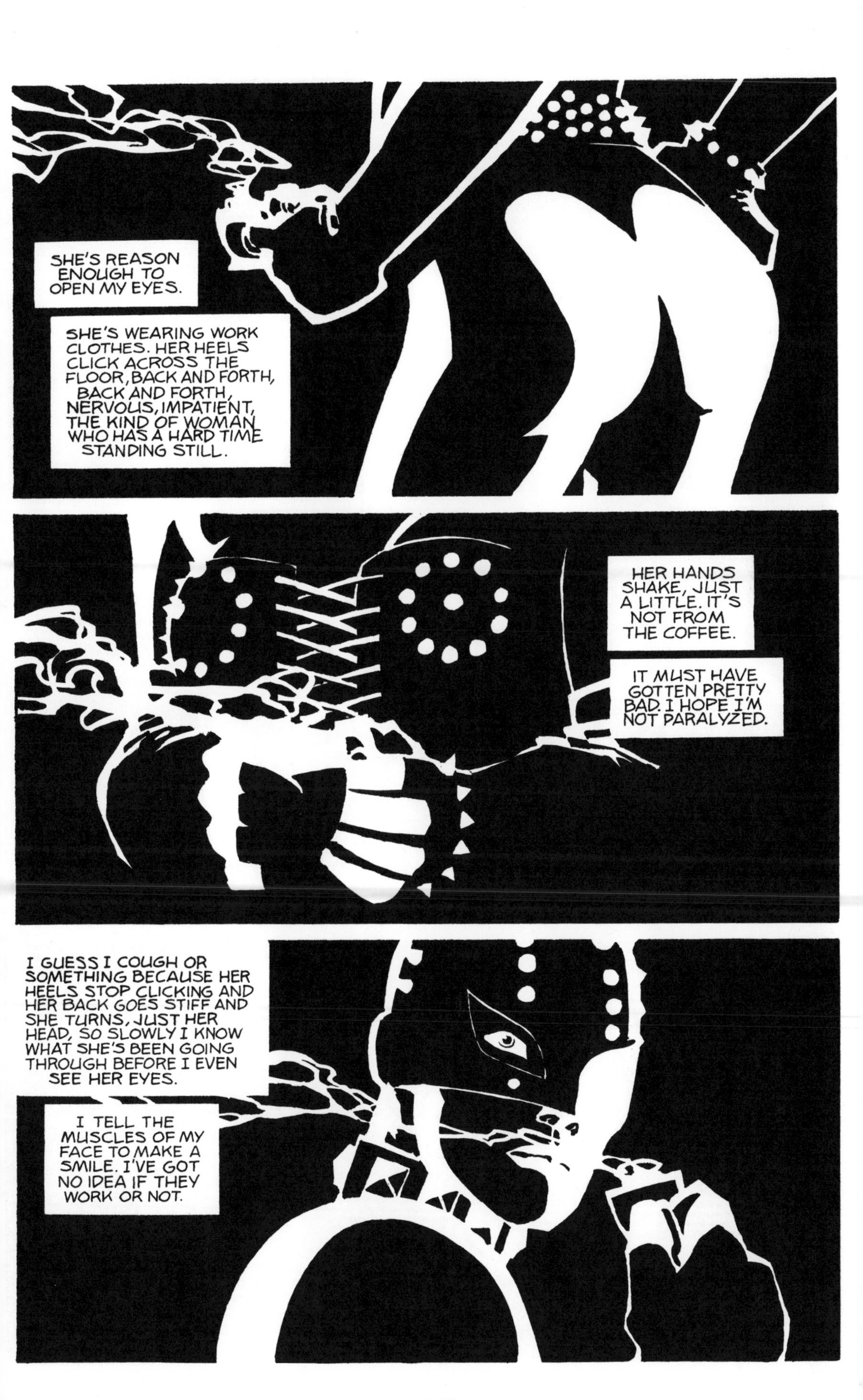
SHE'S REASON ENOUGH TO OPEN MY EYES.
SHE'S WEARING WORK CLOTHES. HER HEELS CLICK ACROSS THE FLOOR, BACK AND FORTH, BACK AND FORTH, NERVOUS, IMPATIENT, THE KIND OF WOMAN WHO HAS A HARD TIME STANDING STILL.
HER HANDS SHAKE, JUST A LITTLE. IT'S NOT FROM THE COFFEE.
IT MUST HAVE GOTTEN PRETTY BAD. I HOPE I'M NOT PARALYZED.
I GUESS I COUGH OR SOMETHING BECAUSE HER HEELS STOP CLICKING AND HER BACK GOES STIFF AND SHE TURNS, JUST HER HEAD, SO SLOWLY I KNOW WHAT SHE'S BEEN GOING THROUGH BEFORE I EVEN SEE HER EYES.
I TELL THE MUSCLES OF MY FACE TO MAKE A SMILE. I'VE GOT NO IDEA IF THEY WORK OR NOT.

CAN YOU HEAR ME, DWIGHT? BLINK YOUR EYES IF YOU CAN HEAR ME... THAT'S GOOD. DON'T TRY TO TALK... YOU'RE GOING TO BE ALL RIGHT, BABY. BUT IT GOT ABOUT AS CLOSE AS IT CAN GET. I WAS SURE YOU WERE DEAD. ONE OF THE BULLETS HIT A PULMONARY ARTERY. YOU WENT INTO CARDIAC ARREST. MOLLY HAD TO CRACK YOUR CHEST OPEN AND REACH RIGHT INSIDE YOU AND MASSAGE YOUR HEART.
NO, BABY. DON'T TRY TO TALK... THE MASK?...
FUNNY. I DIDN'T REALIZE I WAS STILL WEARING IT. I GUESS I'M TIRED. THE TWINS HAVE BEEN WORKING US PRETTY HARD. A COUPLE OF GIRLS HAVE VANISHED. WE'VE BEEN WORKING SIXTEEN-HOUR SHIFTS, BUT WE HAVEN'T A CLUE. IT'S GOT EVERYBODY ON EDGE.
THE TWINS... THAT'S RIGHT, YOU WOULDN'T KNOW THEM. THEY ONLY TOOK CHARGE A FEW WEEKS AGO.
I'M AFRAID YOU'LL BE MEETING THEM, BEFORE LONG. THE COPS WANT YOU PRETTY BADLY. BUT DON'T WORRY. WE'LL FIGURE SOMETHING OUT.
AND WE'LL FIX YOU UP AND GET YOU ON YOUR FEET SO I CAN DECK YOU FOR LEAVING IN THE FIRST PLACE.

MY WARRIOR WOMAN GOES ALL SOFT, SOBBING. *"I TOLD YOU YOU'D BE BACK,"* SHE CROAKS, *"I TOLD YOU YOU BELONG HERE, YOU JERK."*
I WAS A FOOL. I THOUGHT THERE WAS A BETTER WORLD OUT THERE. I THOUGHT I COULD BE A PART OF IT.
I WAS WRONG BOTH TIMES.

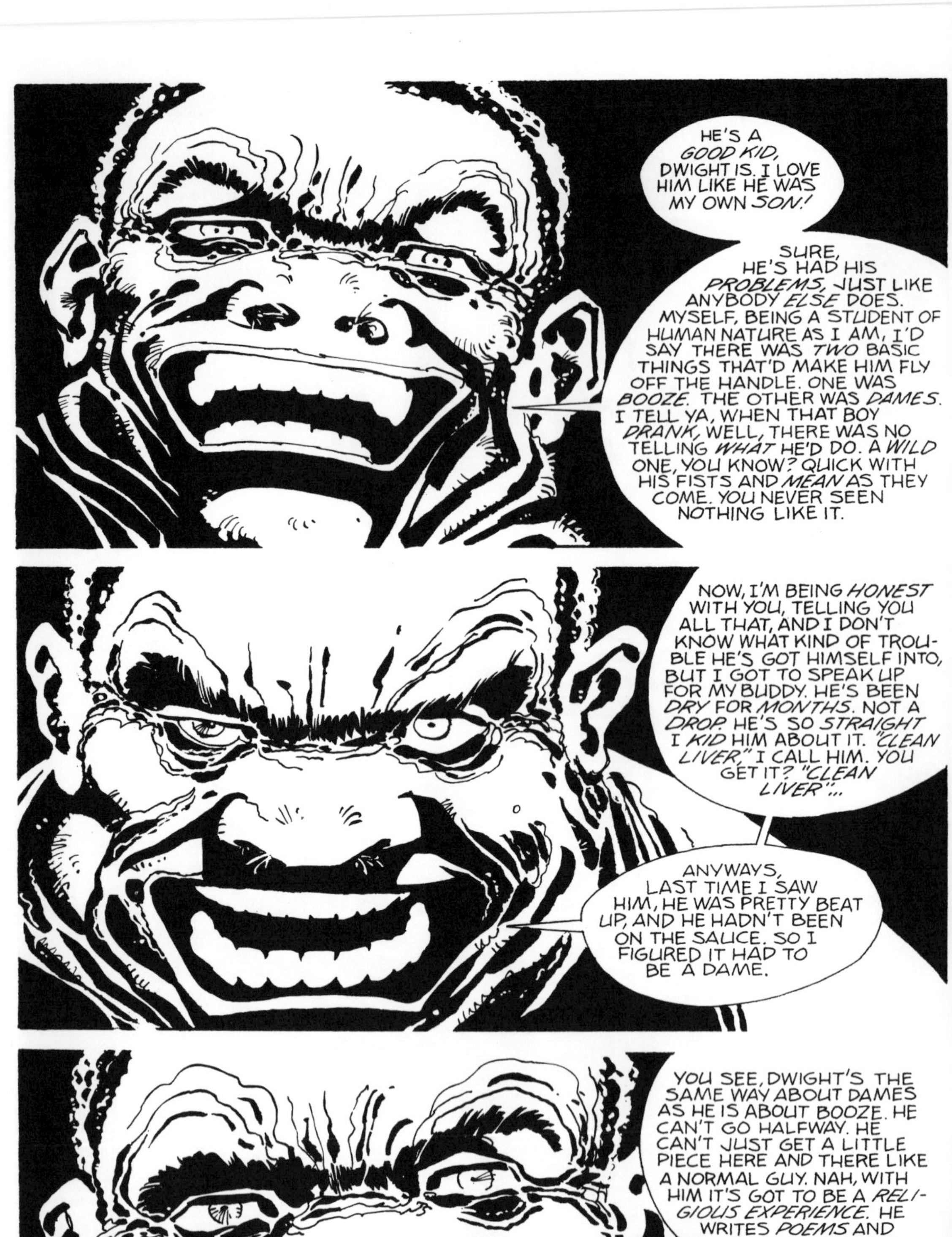
HE'S A GOOD KID, DWIGHT IS. I LOVE HIM LIKE HE WAS MY OWN SON!
SURE, HE'S HAD HIS PROBLEMS, JUST LIKE ANYBODY ELSE DOES. MYSELF, BEING A STUDENT OF HUMAN NATURE AS I AM, I'D SAY THERE WAS TWO BASIC THINGS THAT'D MAKE HIM FLY OFF THE HANDLE. ONE WAS BOOZE. THE OTHER WAS DAMES. I TELL YA, WHEN THAT BOY DRANK, WELL, THERE WAS NO TELLING WHAT HE'D DO. A WILD ONE, YOU KNOW? QUICK WITH HIS FISTS AND MEAN AS THEY COME. YOU NEVER SEEN NOTHING LIKE IT.
NOW, I'M BEING HONEST WITH YOU, TELLING YOU ALL THAT, AND I DON'T KNOW WHAT KIND OF TROUBLE HE'S GOT HIMSELF INTO, BUT I GOT TO SPEAK UP FOR MY BUDDY. HE'S BEEN DRY FOR MONTHS. NOT A DROP. HE'S SO STRAIGHT I KID HIM ABOUT IT. "CLEAN LIVER," I CALL HIM. YOU GET IT? "CLEAN LIVER"...
ANYWAYS, LAST TIME I SAW HIM, HE WAS PRETTY BEAT UP, AND HE HADN'T BEEN ON THE SAUCE. SO I FIGURED IT HAD TO BE A DAME.

YOU SEE, DWIGHT'S THE SAME WAY ABOUT DAMES AS HE IS ABOUT BOOZE. HE CAN'T GO HALFWAY. HE CAN'T JUST GET A LITTLE PIECE HERE AND THERE LIKE A NORMAL GUY. NAH, WITH HIM IT'S GOT TO BE A RELIGIOUS EXPERIENCE. HE WRITES POEMS AND STUFF, LIKE HE DID ABOUT THAT AVA BROAD.
SO HE'S A LITTLE CRAZY THAT WAY AND IF HE'S GOTTEN IN A FIGHT OR SOMETHING, I HOPE YOU'LL SHOW HIM A LITTLE UNDERSTANDING.

NOT TO CHANGE THE SUBJECT, BUT YOU GOT ANY DOUGHNUTS AROUND HERE? EVERYBODY KNOWS ABOUT COPS AND DOUGHNUTS AND I'D GIVE MY RIGHT NUT FOR A COUPLE OF CREAM HORNS.

GET THE MAN SOME CREAM HORNS, BOB.
SIR, McCARTHY MUST HAVE HAD DRINKING BUDDIES. FAVORITE JOINTS HE WENT TO. WE'LL NEED A LIST.

FIRST PIZZA AND NOW IT'S CREAM HORNS...
DRINKING BUDDIES? NAH, NOT DWIGHT! HE'S A LONER--AND THAT'S ANOTHER ONE OF HIS PROBLEMS. HE SPENDS TOO MUCH TIME BY HIMSELF. IT JUST AIN'T NATURAL. I TELL YA, I COULD WRITE A BOOK...

MOLLY SAYS YOU'RE READY TO LEAVE.

NO. I'M STAYING.

WRONG ANSWER.
ALL SIX FEET OF GAIL ARE READY TO SPRING INTO ACTION. BUT IT'S NOT THE .45 SHE'S HIDING THAT I'M COUNTING ON.
SHE WOULDN'T STAND A CHANCE AGAINST MIHO.

DEADLY LITTLE MIHO.
IF SHE RECOGNIZES ME, SHE DOESN'T LET IT SHOW.

MISTER, I DON'T KNOW IF YOU'RE CRAZY OR STUPID OR BOTH, BUT YOU PICKED THE WRONG NEIGHBORHOOD FOR YOUR HIDEOUT. IF GAIL HADN'T RAISED A STINK, YOU'D BE IN THE MORGUE RIGHT NOW.
ALIVE OR DEAD, YOU'RE LEAVING.
I'M STAYING.

YOU'LL STONE-WALL THE COPS. YOU'LL PROVIDE THE SERVICES OF GAIL, MIHO, AND MOLLY.
WHEN I GIVE AN ORDER, IT WILL BE OBEYED.

I SHOULD FEAR FOR MY LIFE, AND I WOULD--
--IF I COULD JUST GET THAT DAMN "DOUBLEMINT" JINGLE OUT OF MY HEAD.

I DON'T THINK HE CAN FEEL IT, MIHO. GIVE IT A TWIST.
OUR FINAL OFFER. WE'LL PACK YOU IN A TRUCK THAT'LL TAKE YOU ALL THE WAY TO SEATTLE--YOU WON'T GIVE WITH ANY MORE MOUTH ABOUT STAYING HERE--
--OR MIHO WILL EXHALE AND THAT HEART MOLLY WORKED SO HARD TO FIX WILL POP LIKE A GRAPE.

GAIL-- TELL THEM ABOUT MANUEL.
YES, DWIGHT.

GAIL FIRES UP ONE OF HER WEIRD RUSSIAN CIGARETTES. SHE TAKES HER TIME TELLING THE STORY.

SHE TELLS THEM ABOUT MANUEL AND HIS FOUR *BROTHERS*-- ABOUT WHAT THEY DID TO *KELLEY* AND *SANDY* AND *DENISE*.

SHE TELLS THEM ABOUT WHAT I DID TO THAT PACK OF WHITE SLAVERS.

SHE GIVES EVERY DETAIL, HER VOICE FLAT, PRECISE, AS IF SHE WERE IN COURT.

JUST WHEN I THINK SHE'S FINISHED, SHE STAMPS OUT HER CIGARETTE AND FREEZES THE ROOM WITH HER VALKYRIE GLARE. SHE SNAPS OFF EACH WORD LIKE A GUNSHOT:

THEY ALL SEEM TO BE WAITING FOR THE OTHER SHOE TO DROP.

SO I DROP IT.
IT WAS VERY DARK, IN THAT ALLEY, THREE YEARS AGO.
THREE OF THE TONG WHO ATTACKED MIHO WERE DEAD BY HER HAND. BUT THE LAST TWO HAD HER DEAD TO RIGHTS. POINT-BLANK RANGE.

IT WAS VERY DARK. SHE PROBABLY DIDN'T GET A GOOD LOOK AT THE MAN WHO SAVED HER.

I GET WHAT I WANT. MORE TIME--

--AND MORE *SURGERY.*

MR. McCARTHY WAS A GOOD TENANT. HE ALWAYS PAID HIS RENT ON TIME. HE WAS QUIET AND POLITE AND HE EVEN FIXED THINGS AROUND THE BUILDING WITHOUT BEING ASKED TO. IF HE'S DONE SOMETHING WRONG, I CAN'T IMAGINE WHAT IT COULD BE.
AND YES, BEFORE YOU ASK, I KNOW HE HAD SOME ROUGH TIMES...
...HE TOLD ME ABOUT ALL THAT WHEN HE APPLIED FOR THE LEASE.
HE KEPT TO HIMSELF. HE NEVER HAD ANY GUESTS-- UNTIL THAT ONE, HORRIBLE NIGHT. I NEVER SHOULD HAVE LET THAT WOMAN IN. BUT SHE WAS SO *BEAUTIFUL* --AND HE ALWAYS SEEMED SO *LONELY*, AND, WELL, I GUESS *YOU* CAN CALL ME A ROMANTIC.
WHEN MR. McCARTHY CAME HOME, HE LOOKED LIKE HE'D BEEN IN A FIGHT. HE SAID HE'D BEEN MUGGED AND I DIDN'T SEE ANY REASON TO DOUBT HIS WORD.
HE WENT TO HIS ROOM AND IT WASN'T LONG BEFORE, WELL... THEY MADE A LOT OF NOISE. THEY WERE HAVING QUITE A TIME. MY LORD, HOW THE CEILING SHOOK. HE KEPT SHOUTING HER NAME--*AVA*, I THINK IT WAS. MIND YOU, IF IT HAD BEEN ANY OTHER TENANT, I WOULD HAVE HAD WORDS WITH HIM.
THEN THE SOUNDS TURNED *VIOLENT*. *POUNDING*. *CRASHING*. BREAKING *GLASS*. THE WOMAN *SCREAMED*...

COME ON, MORT! THIS STINKS TO HIGH HEAVEN! SHE WENT TO HIS APARTMENT-- THAT SAME NIGHT!
WE HAVEN'T HEARD AVA'S SIDE OF IT YET, HAVE WE? FOR ALL WE KNOW THE LANDLADY'S IN ON IT WITH McCARTHY.

IN ON WHAT? FIRST THE GUY'S A PSYCHO KILLER--NOW HE'S MASTERMINDING A CONSPIRACY? THERE'S ONLY ONE PERSON WHO HAD ANYTHING TO GAIN FROM DAMIEN LORD GETTING KILLED--
--AND YOU'RE TOO BUSY BANGING THE BROAD TO BRING HER IN FOR QUESTIONING!
YOU DON'T KNOW HER! YOU DON'T KNOW ANYTHING ABOUT HER! AND I'LL BE DAMNED IF I'LL LET YOU USE THAT KIND OF LANGUAGE WHEN YOU TALK ABOUT HER!

OH, CHRIST. YOU SCHMUCK. YOU STUPID SCHMUCK. YOU'RE IN LOVE WITH HER.
JESUS, MAN. IT'S ONE THING TO POKE A BABE ON THE SIDE, BUT THIS IS THE WORST. YOU CAN'T EVEN THINK STRAIGHT.
SHUT THE HELL UP! I'M WARNING YOU! JUST SHUT THE HELL UP! I KNOW WHAT I'M DOING!

DARLING ...OH, DARLING...
AVA...

...I LIVE FOR THESE MOMENTS. I ONLY WISH-- I KNOW IT'S SELFISH, BUT I WISH YOU COULD STAY ALL NIGHT. JUST ONCE...
...WHAT IS IT? WHAT'S WRONG? SOMETHING'S WRONG. I CAN TELL.
McCARTHY'S LANDLADY. SHE SAID YOU WENT TO SEE HIM. AT HIS APARTMENT. THE NIGHT OF THE MURDER.

YES. I WENT TO HIM. AND HE RAPED ME. AND HE ALMOST KILLED ME.

I THOUGHT I COULD REASON WITH HIM. CALM HIM DOWN. BUT HE WAS WORSE THAN EVER. HE STRUCK ME. HE THREW ME TO THE FLOOR. HE TOOK ME, HIS HANDS AT MY THROAT, STRANGLING ME WHILE HE... THE WHOLE TIME. IF MANUTE HADN'T FOL-LOWED ME...

OH, GOD! IT'S ALL MY FAULT! IF I HADN'T GONE THERE--HE MIGHT HAVE STAYED AWAY! AND NOW --NOW NOTHING WILL STOP HIM!
HE'LL KILL ME! EVEN IF YOU CATCH HIM! HE'LL FIND A WAY! HE'LL KILL ME!

NO, AVA. HE'LL NEVER HURT YOU AGAIN. BECAUSE I'M GOING TO KILL HIM. I SWEAR I WILL.

I'LL GIVE YOU CREDIT FOR ONE THING, MORT.

YOU TAKE ME TO ALL THE BEST PLACES.
YAAA
KRUNCH
AND YOU--YOUR COAT LOOKS LIKE BAGHDAD. SO'S YOUR FACE. TAKE OFF.

WE'RE POLICE OFFICERS. WE NEED TO SPEAK TO A MEMBER OF YOUR STAFF.
OKAY. SURE. WHAT-EVER.
HE'S NEW HERE, MARV. HE DIDN'T KNOW.
THAT'S OKAY, JOSIE. NO BLOOD, NO FOUL.

WE'RE LOOKING FOR A WAITRESS NAMED SHELLIE.
SURE, OFFICER. GRAB YOURSELF A TABLE AND I'LL SEND HER OVER. BUT DON'T GO SHOWING OFF YOUR BADGES-- AND KEEP IN MIND WE'RE PAID UP.
...DIDN'T MEAN IT LORD I DIDN'T MEAN IT I DON'T KNOW WHAT GOT INTO ME YOU KNOW I LOVE YOU, DARLING...
MORT, IF I SAID ANYTHING BAD ABOUT THIS PLACE, I TAKE IT BACK.
JUST *LOOK* AT THAT DOLL...

I'M SHELLIE. THIS ISN'T ABOUT THAT STUPID *BROTHER* OF MINE, IS IT?
NO, MA'AM.
DAMN...
JUST DON'T GO SHOWING OFF YOUR BADGES--AND KEEP IN MIND WE'RE PAID UP.
YES, MA'AM. YOU WERE SEEN WITH *DWIGHT McCARTHY...*

DWIGHT McCARTHY? WHAT KIND OF MESS HAS THAT JERK GOT HIMSELF INTO?
NO. NEVER MIND. DON'T TELL ME. I DON'T WANT TO HEAR ABOUT IT. I BARELY KNOW THE CREEP--AND WHAT I DO KNOW, I DON'T LIKE. LOUSY TIPPER--NIGHT AFTER NIGHT HE'D JUST SIT THERE, TOSSING THEM BACK AND LOOKING LIKE A LOST PUPPY. AT LEAST HE KEPT TO HIMSELF--UNTIL THAT NIGHT I FELT SORRY FOR HIM AND WE STARTED TALKING.
TALKING. THAT, HE WAS GOOD AT. FROM ANYBODY ELSE IT WOULD'VE BEEN THE USUAL "SHE DONE ME WRONG," BUT FROM HIM, IT--WELL, IT GOT TO ME, YOU KNOW?
I WAS A SUCKER. I TOOK HIM HOME WITH ME. YEAH, IT WAS MY IDEA. I'VE HAD BETTER ONES.
ONE THING LED TO ANOTHER AND ONCE HE GOT GOING, HE WAS A WILD ONE, I'LL TELL YOU THAT. IT WAS SOMETHING ELSE--UNTIL THE JERK STARTED CALLING OUT HER NAME. AVA, IT WAS. IT'S EASY TO REMEMBER. HE MUST'VE SAID IT FIFTEEN TIMES. THEN ALL OF A SUDDEN HE STARTED BAWLING AND HE RAN OUT. HE DIDN'T EVEN SAY GOODBYE. HE DIDN'T EVEN HAVE THE BALLS TO APOLOGIZE.
SO SIX MONTHS GO BY. SIX MONTHS AND NOT SO MUCH AS A PHONE CALL. THEN IN HE WALKS, HIS FACE ALL PUNCHED IN, JUST STINKING OF BOOZE--BUT IT TURNED OUT HE WAS JUST GETTING STARTED. I SWEAR, EVEN HIM I NEVER SAW HIT THE BOTTLE SO HARD. DRINKING ALONE, JUST LIKE ALWAYS. AND HE LEFT ALONE, TOO. WHO'D HAVE THE STOMACH TO GO ANYWHERE WITH HIM WHEN HE'S LIKE THAT?
HE PROBABLY CRAWLED OFF TO OLD TOWN--AND INTO ANOTHER BOTTLE. HE'S GOT FRIENDS IN OLD TOWN, IF YOU KNOW WHAT I MEAN.

THUMP
TAKE IT EASY, WEEVIL. I'M HERE TO DO YOU A FAVOR. IT'S MONEY IN YOUR POCKET.
HE *WAS* LAST SEEN IN OLD TOWN...
DON'T EVEN *THINK* ABOUT IT. IT'S YOUR *CAREER*-- AND YOUR *LIFE*.

SPREAD THE WORD, WEEVIL. AND GET GOOD CASH FOR IT BECAUSE IT'S WORTH IT.
TELL THEM I'VE BEEN HITTING THE JOINTS, DRUNK OFF MY BUTT, CRYING OVER SOME HOT BABE NAME OF GOLDIE.
KRNCH
HHUKK
GHAAK
DWIGHT, IT'S SHELLIE. THE COPS WERE JUST HERE. YEAH, I HANDLED IT LIKE YOU TOLD ME TO. YOU TAKE CARE OF YOURSELF, WILD MAN.

WHAT'LL IT BE, MARV?
A SHOT AND A BREW, SHELLIE. THANKS.

BRINGG!

CHAPTER
EIGHT

AVA. YOU CAN'T MEAN THIS. NOT AFTER EVERYTHING WE'VE MEANT TO EACH OTHER.
IT'S TEARING MY HEART OUT, MORT! BUT I JUST CAN'T STAND IT ANYMORE! DWIGHT IS STILL OUT THERE! HE'S GOING TO KILL ME! AND YOU KNOW WHERE HE IS! AND YOU WON'T DO A DAMN THING ABOUT IT! HOW CAN I TRULY BELIEVE YOU LOVE ME? WE'RE THROUGH, MORT! IT'S OVER!
YOU DON'T KNOW WHAT YOU'RE ASKING. WE HAVE TO WAIT FOR HIM TO COME OUT OF OLD TOWN. IT'S THE ONLY WAY.
LISTEN TO YOU! YOU'RE A SIN CITY COP! YOU'VE GOT A BADGE AND A GUN! YOU'VE GOT POWER! USE IT!
IF YOU EVER WANT TO HAVE THIS WOMAN AGAIN--BE A MAN!

WAKE UP. DON'T MOVE.

McCARTHY. THE DEATH-- ALREADY, IT'S IN YOUR EYES. YOU BREATHE AND THINK AND SPEAK BUT YOUR SOUL IS DEAD. THE BODY WILL FOLLOW.

OH, I'M FIT ENOUGH. I'M READY TO SETTLE THE SCORE. BUT FIRST, THERE'S A COUPLE OF THINGS I'VE GOT TO BE CLEAR ON--ALL THAT TALK ABOUT *TORTURE,* YOU TWO COOKED THAT UP, RIGHT? YOU'RE HER *LOVER*.
FOOL! THE GODDESS TAKES NO *LOVER*. THE GODDESS MAKES *SLAVES* OF MEN. DAMIEN LORD. YOU. ME. WE SERVE. WHEN SHE WISHES, WE DIE. IT IS THAT SIMPLE.

"GODDESS"? SPARE ME, WILL YOU? I CAN THINK OF A WHOLE PILE OF NAMES TO CALL HER, BUT GODDESS ISN'T ONE OF THEM.
NEXT QUESTION. HOW MANY OTHERS, MANUTE? HOW MANY MEN HAS SHE TRICKED AND RUINED AND MURDERED?
DOZENS. IT'S SO EASY FOR HER. IN AN INSTANT, SHE CAN SEE TO THE HEART OF YOU--AND TRANSFORM HERSELF INTO YOUR DEEPEST DESIRE. TO DAMIEN LORD, SHE WAS A PRINCESS BRIDE. TO YOU, SHE WAS A DAMSEL IN DISTRESS. NONE OF YOU EVER HAD A CHANCE.
SHE DEVOURED YOU, ALL OF YOU. SOMETIMES FOR PROFIT. SOMETIMES FOR SPORT. THERE WAS A PRIEST SHE DROVE TO SUICIDE. THERE WAS AN ARTIST, A GENIUS--HIS MASTERPIECE WAS A SCULPTURE OF AVA. NOW HE WANDERS THE STREETS, INSANE. YOU CANNOT HARM HER, DEAD MAN. YOU CANNOT STOP HER. SHE IS THE GODDESS. SHE CANNOT DIE.
YOU'RE AS CRAZY AS SHE IS. IF YOU WERE AS ROTTEN AS HER, I'D BLOW YOUR BRAINS OUT RIGHT NOW. BUT I'M TRYING TO BE CAREFUL ABOUT WHO I KILL, AND ALL YOU DID WAS POUND THE CRAP OUT OF ME. YOU'VE ALREADY PAID AN EYE FOR THAT SO I'M LETTING YOU OFF WITH A WARNING. STAY IN THAT BED. DON'T GO BACK TO WORK. DON'T GET IN MY WAY.
HIS CHUCKLE IS LIKE ROLLING THUNDER.
HE'S LAUGHING OUT LOUD BY THE TIME I LEAVE.

NO, AVA. YOU'RE NO GODDESS. YOU'RE A WITCH, A PREDATOR. MAYBE I ONLY GOT WHAT I DESERVED-- BUT WHAT ABOUT THE OTHERS? GOOD MEN, DRIVEN MAD...
THAT DOES IT, MORT. YOU HAVE REALLY LOST IT! BAD ENOUGH YOU LEAVE YOUR WIFE FOR THAT BROAD--NOW YOU'RE THROWING AWAY YOUR CAREER!
I KNOW WHAT I'M DOING, BOB! HOW MANY TIMES DO I HAVE TO TELL YOU THAT? I'M GOING TO OLD TOWN! I'M GOING TO NAIL THIS GUY ONCE AND FOR ALL! IF I HAVE TO GO IT ALONE, I WILL!
TURN THE CAR AROUND, MORT. WE'RE HEADING BACK TO THE STATION. YOU'VE GOT TO COME CLEAN WITH THE CAPTAIN.
COME CLEAN ABOUT WHAT? I'M A COP. I'M DOING MY JOB. I'M HUNTING DOWN A MURDERER.
OH, GIVE ME A BREAK! YOU'RE SCREWING UP EVERY WAY THERE IS! YOU'VE GOT TO DITCH THAT DAME!
THAT'S ENOUGH, BOB. WE WON'T TALK ABOUT AVA. DON'T PUSH IT.
LEV311

SOMEBODY'S GOT TO SET YOU STRAIGHT! FORGET THAT STUPID WHORE AND TURN THE CAR AROUND!
SHUT THE HELL UP, YOU FAT LITTLE BASTARD! I'M GOING TO OLD TOWN! I'M GOING TO FIND McCARTHY AND KILL HIM BEFORE HE COMES AFTER THE WOMAN I LOVE!
I'M GOING TO DO WHAT I'M GOING TO DO AND IF YOU TRY TO STOP ME YOU'RE MAKING A BIG MISTAKE! A REALLY BIG MISTAKE! I MEAN IT!

SO NOW IT'S THREATS! YOU'RE OUT OF YOUR MIND! TURN THE CAR AROUND OR I'M TURNING YOU IN!
I WARNED YOU! EVERY DAY I WARNED YOU! BUT YOU KEEP ASKING FOR IT AND ASKING FOR IT! WELL HERE IT IS, PAL!

MORT-- NO--
BLAM!

BLAM!!

WHUFF

BLAM

A WITCH. A PREDATOR.
DESTROYING LIVES.
SOMETIMES FOR *PROFIT*.
SOMETIMES FOR *SPORT*.

BUT NOW YOU'RE LOCKED AWAY IN YOUR MANSION, SURROUNDED BY MEN AND GUNS. A BIRD OF PREY IN A GILDED CAGE.
YOU'VE HAD MONTHS TO WAIT AND WONDER AND WORRY. IS IT GETTING TO YOU YET? ARE YOU READY TO DO SOMETHING STUPID?
I'M SO HAPPY YOU CHOSE TO ATTEND MY LITTLE PARTY, MR. WALLENQUIST. I'M WELL AWARE YOUR DEALINGS WITH MY HUSBAND WERE LESS THAN SATISFYING.
TRUE. I WAS SURPRISED BY YOUR INVITATION. I HAD ASSUMED YOU SHARED LORD'S DISTASTE FOR MATTERS EXTRALEGAL. IT TOOK SEVERAL PHONE CALLS TO DETERMINE WHY YOU SOUGHT MY ATTENTION.
I'M FLATTERED THAT A MAN LIKE YOU WOULD SHOW SUCH INTEREST.

I'LL WARN YOU ONCE AND ONCE ONLY, MRS. LORD--DO NOT FLIRT WITH ME. I HAVE NO USE FOR YOUR CHARMS.
YOU'RE AN AMATEUR IN A GAME BEST LEFT TO PROFESSIONALS. YOU'VE ENJOYED AN AMATEUR'S LUCK. BUT THE TWO POLICEMEN--THAT WAS AN EMBARRASSING BLUNDER. YOU NEED THIS CASE SETTLED. YOU NEED DWIGHT McCARTHY'S CORPSE AND A SUICIDE NOTE IN WHICH HE CONFESSES TO THE MURDER OF DAMIEN LORD.
I WILL PROVIDE THESE THINGS. MY PRICE FOR DOING SO WILL BE FAR HIGHER THAN THE RATHER OBVIOUS ONE YOU SEEM SO FOND OF PAYING.

AS OF NOW, OUR CORPORATIONS ARE IN PARTNERSHIP.
MY AGENT WILL ARRIVE TOMORROW NIGHT. FROM PHOENIX. BY TRAIN.

THE 10:46 FROM PHOENIX LUMBERS INTO BASIN CITY CENTRAL, DEAD ON TIME.

GOOD EVENING, SIR. WE HAVE A CAR WAITING. I'LL TAKE YOUR BAG.
WRONG BOTH TIMES, BUDDY. NOBODY TOUCHES MY GEAR--AND I GOT SOMEBODY PICKING ME UP WHO'S ONE HELL OF A LOT CUTER THAN YOU.

IT WAS OUR UNDERSTANDING THAT YOU WOULD BE *ALONE*.
LIVE WITH IT, BIG GUY. I'M FULL OF SURPRISES.

EDDIE!
SHAKE YOUR WAY OVER TO THE SHOTGUN SIDE, DOLL. I'M DRIVING.

CAN WE GO DANCING, EDDIE? I FEEL CRAZY TONIGHT. I CAN'T SETTLE DOWN.
SURE, BABY. DANCING. TABLES. THE WORKS. YOU DON'T VISIT SIN CITY TO READ THE BIBLE. BUT FIRST I GOT ME A MEETING TO DO. IT WON'T TAKE A HALF-HOUR.

DHV
DHV
DO YOU THINK HE SUSPECTS?
NO WAY OF KNOWING.

HURRY BACK, EDDIE. YOU KNOW I GET IMPATIENT-- AND YOU KNOW I GET A LITTLE CRAZY WHEN I GET IMPATIENT.
AND YOU KNOW I GET JEALOUS. DON'T BE STUPID. REMEMBER PHILLY.
KEEP AN EYE ON THE WOMAN, BOOGAARD.
YES, SIR!

I FIGURE WE GOT US A GOOD *TWENTY MINUTES* ON OUR HANDS WITH *NOTHING* TO DO. I *HATE* JUST SITTING STILL, DON'T YOU?

SOMETIMES EDDIE ISN'T FAIR AT ALL. LIKE RIGHT NOW, TO TAKE A FOR INSTANCE. HE SHOULDN'T HAVE LEFT ME ALL ALONE WITH A GUY LIKE *YOU*. YOU'RE SO *TALL*. I *LIKE* TALL GUYS. THEY MAKE ME WANT TO DO ALL KINDS OF *CRAZY* THINGS. BUT YOU AND ME, IF WE WAS TO GO AND DO SOMETHING WE *SHOULDN'T*, EDDIE, HE'D KILL BOTH OF US IF HE WAS TO FIND OUT. LAST TIME HE HURT ME *REALLY BAD*.

SO HE BETTER NOT FIND OUT. THAT'S IF WE DO SOMETHING WE SHOULDN'T.
MY LIPS ARE *SEALED*.

KRAKK

MRS. LORD IS BATHING. SHE WILL BE READY TO ENTERTAIN YOU MOMENTARILY.
JACOBY. KILL THIS MAN IF HE MOVES.
YES, SIR.
WHAT *IS* THIS CRAP?

JUST LIKE THAT, EVERYTHING GOES RIGHT STRAIGHT TO HELL.
IF THEY *STRIP-SEARCH* ME, I'M *FINISHED*.
MY COMPLIMENTS TO YOUR SURGEON, MR. McCARTHY. A REMARKABLE TRANSFORMATION. BUT YOU STILL HAVE THE *EYES*. THE EYES OF A DEAD MAN.

THUNK
GYAAA!

KLIKK

BATHING. I SHOULD'VE KNOWN SHE'D BE BATHING.
I USED TO KID HER, ABOUT ALL HER SWIMMING AND BATHING. I SAID SHE WAS PART FISH. MY LITTLE MERMAID.
THAT WAS A LONG TIME AGO. BACK WHEN WE WERE LOVERS.
A LONG TIME AGO.

AVA.
DAMN.

SHE FINALLY COMES UP FOR AIR. MANUTE TELLS HER WHO I AM.

PLINT

DWIGHT... IT'S *TRUE.* IT'S *YOU.* AMAZING. YOU WENT TO ALL THIS TROUBLE-- OVER *ME?*
WHATEVER DID YOU DO WITH THE MAN WHO WAS *SUPPOSED* TO BE ON THAT TRAIN?
SHE KEEPS TALKING BUT I CAN'T HEAR IT PAST THE POUNDING IN MY EARS. MY JAW'S SO TIGHT IT FEELS LIKE IT'S GOING TO POP FROM MY SKULL. MY BACK IS IN KNOTS. I'VE BEEN *MADE* AND I'VE DRAGGED MIHO AND GAIL INTO THIS WITH ME.
NO. DON'T THINK THAT WAY. BREATHE STEADY. RELAX INTO IT. IF YOU GET THE OPENING YOU'RE COUNTING ON, BE READY FOR IT.
LET'S JUST SAY HE NEVER LEFT PHOENIX.

STEAM STILL RISES FROM HER SKIN.
EVERYTHING SHE'S DONE AND I STILL CAN'T TAKE MY EYES OFF HER.
EVERYTHING SHE'S DONE. OVER ALL THE YEARS. ALL THE LIES AND TEARS AND BLOOD AND DEATH, AND STILL I CAN'T TAKE MY EYES OFF HER.
AND DOESN'T SHE KNOW IT. SHE SMILES AND STRUTS, SHOWING IT OFF, TURNING EVERY MAGNIFICENT INCH OF HERSELF IN THE LIGHT.

THINK. CONCENTRATE. FEEL THE WEIGHT OF THE COLD THING NESTLED IN YOUR SLEEVE, STRAPPED TO YOUR LEFT ARM.
RELAX. THINK. CONCENTRATE.

*REMEMBER WHAT SHE **DID.** REMEMBER WHAT SHE **IS.** LET HER TALK. WAIT FOR YOUR **OPENING.***
WAIT FOR GAIL TO DO HER BIT...

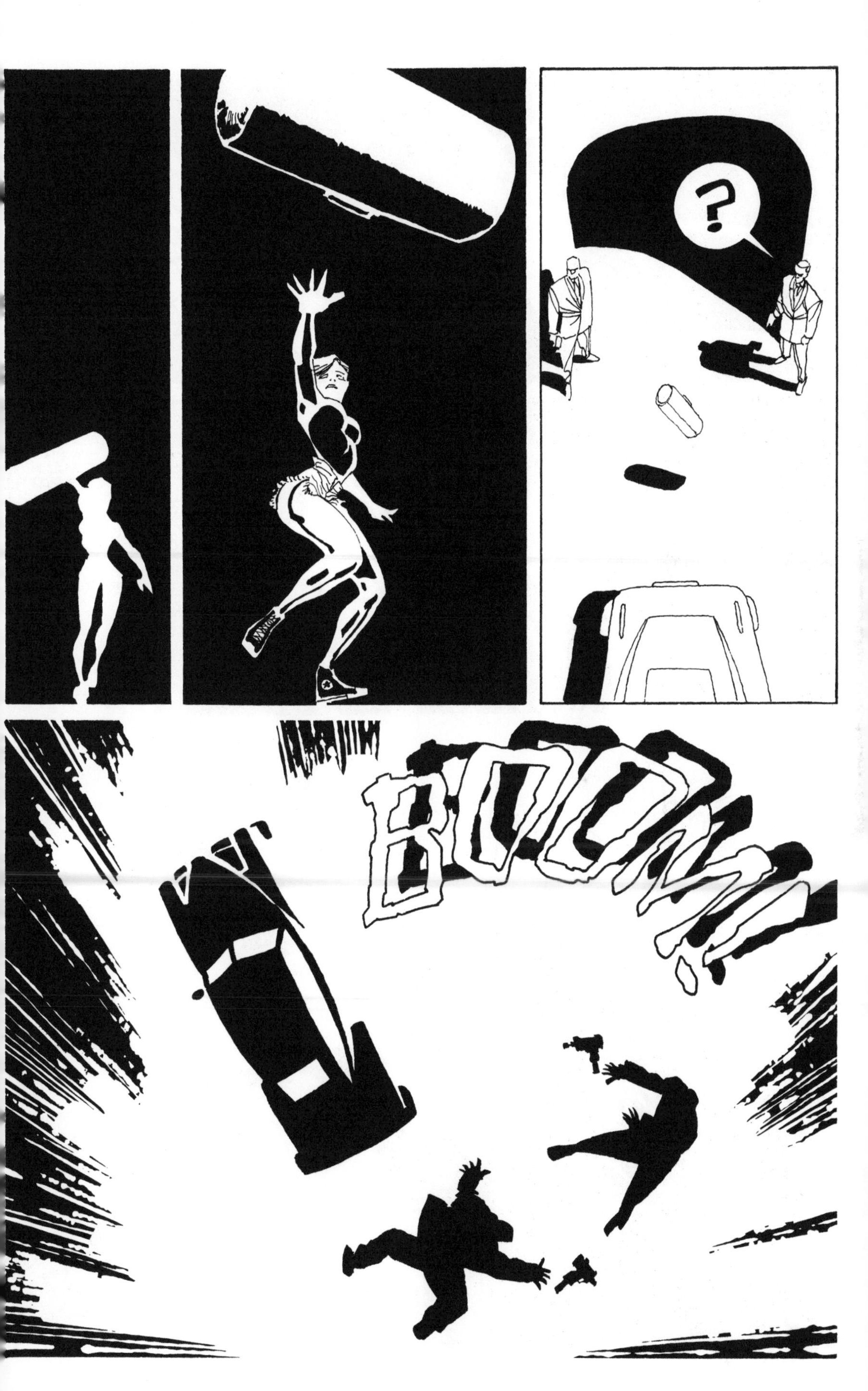
?
BOOOM!

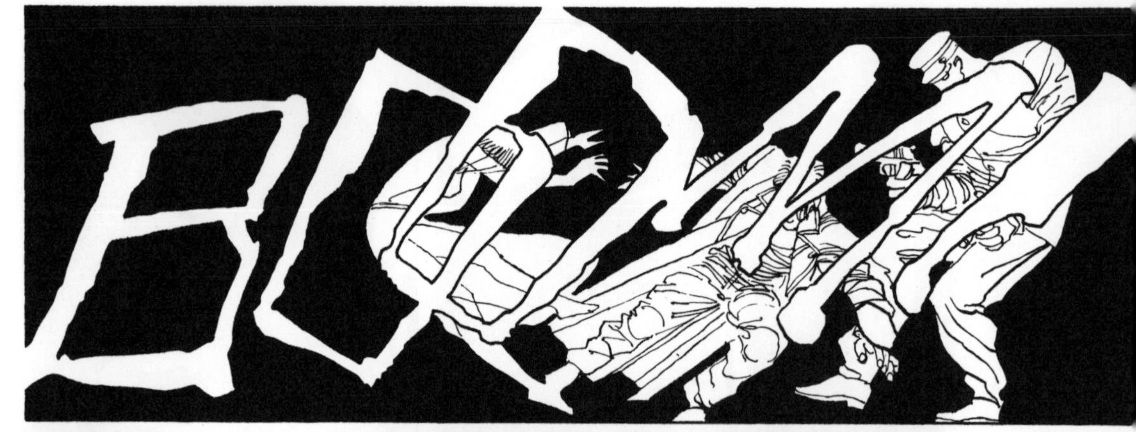
BOOM

SNAKK
ALARMS GO OFF ALL OVER THE PLACE. MEN SHOUT. MACHINE PISTOLS RATTLE AT RANDOM. ALL HELL IS BREAKING LOOSE OUT THERE. THE GIRLS HAVE GIVEN ME ONE CLEAR CHANCE.
IT'S JUST A CRUMMY LITTLE .25. THAT'S ALL I COULD FIT UP MY SLEEVE.

POW!
POW!
POW!

POW!
POW!
POW!

STUPID. SIX SHOTS-- AND NOT A SINGLE HEAD WOUND...
KHOF

BLAM!

THEN IT ALL GETS DOWN TO SPEED AND LUCK.

SHE'S PANTING, SOBBING.
HER EYES ARE WET AND FULL OF LOVE.

BEHIND ME --A GROWL. HE'LL BE ON ME IN SECONDS.
THIS'LL BE TRICKY.

DWIGHT! GET DOWN!
BLAM

GODDESS
GYARR
I GUESS SHE FIGURED I WAS THE WINNING HORSE.

HURGG
IT'S A LITTLE *LATE* IN THE *RACE* TO CHANGE YOUR *BET*, AVA.

HEFF

CRASH

HNH?

DEADLY LITTLE MIHO.
A FALLING LEAF WOULD MAKE MORE NOISE.

THUNK! THUNK!

KILL HIM. TELL HER TO KILL HIM. IT'S THE ONLY WAY. IT WAS HIM. ALL ALONG. TELL HER TO CHOP HIS GOD DAMNED HEAD OFF! IT WAS HIM! HE'S NOT HUMAN! HE CONTROLLED MY MIND!
STOP IT, AVA. NO MORE LIES. IT'S OVER.

IT'S NOT A LIE! NOT THIS TIME! OH, DWIGHT --I CAN'T BLAME YOU IF YOU DON'T BELIEVE ME, BUT I BEG YOU TO HEAR ME OUT. IT WOULD BE SUCH A CRUEL IRONY IF THINGS ENDED THIS WAY.
IT ALL BEGAN THREE YEARS AGO...
SHE GOES ON. I DON'T LOOK INTO HER EYES. THAT HELPS A LITTLE BIT.
...MANUTE USED ANCIENT TECHNIQUES--ANCIENT MYSTICISM. HE CRAWLED INSIDE OUR MINDS. HE TOOK CONTROL OF DAMIEN'S EMPIRE... OH, GOD, IT'S SUCH A BLUR ...DAMIEN BEGAN TO FIGHT HIM. HE WAS GOING TO EXPOSE MANUTE AS THE MONSTER HE IS. SO MANUTE USED ME. I TRIED TO FIGHT, BUT I WAS WEAK, SO WEAK...
THEN SHE PULLS CLOSE AND I'VE GOT TO LOOK AND ALL I WANT IS TO BE LOST IN THE SIGHT AND SOUND AND SMELL OF HER...
MY LOVE --IT WOULD BE HIS FINAL TRIUMPH IF WE LOST EACH OTHER NOW. I'M FREE. FREE OF DAMIEN. FREE OF MANUTE. WE CAN BE HAPPY. TOGETHER. FOREVER.
HER KISS IS A PROMISE OF PARADISE.

THE GUN BARKS AND BUCKS IN MY HAND. LIFE LEAVES AVA WITH A SIGH.
SIRENS CLIMB THE HILL. DOWN IN THE COURTYARD GAIL HONKS THE HORN, IMPATIENT.
WE'LL TAKE THE BACK ROADS, THE OLD BOOTLEGGER ROADS.
THEY'LL NEVER CATCH US.
THE END

FOR
CYCLONE

GRAPHIC NOVELS BY FRANK MILLER

AVAILABLE FROM DARK HORSE BOOKS

FRANK MILLER'S *SIN CITY* SERIES

THE HARD GOODBYE
ISBN 978-1-59307-293-3
$19.00

A DAME TO KILL FOR
ISBN 978-1-59307-294-0
$19.00

THE BIG FAT KILL
ISBN 978-1-59307-295-7
$19.00

THAT YELLOW BASTARD
ISBN 978-1-59307-296-4
$21.00

FAMILY VALUES
ISBN 978-1-59307-297-1
$14.00

BOOZE, BROADS, & BULLETS
ISBN 978-1-59307-298-8
$17.00

HELL AND BACK
ISBN 978-1-59307-299-5
$30.00

THE ART OF SIN CITY
ISBN 978-1-61655-247-3
$25.00

OTHER WORKS

300
with Lynn Varley
ISBN 978-1-56971-402-7
$30.00

THE BIG GUY AND RUSTY THE BOY ROBOT
drawn by Geof Darrow
ISBN 978-1-56971-201-6
$14.95

HARD BOILED
drawn by Geof Darrow
ISBN 978-1-87857-458-9
$16.95

THE LIFE AND TIMES OF MARTHA WASHINGTON IN THE TWENTY-FIRST CENTURY
drawn by Dave Gibbons
ISBN 978-1-59582-482-0
$29.99

SIN CITY
A DAME TO KILL FOR
SIN CITY
2 OF 6
$2.95 US
$3.70 CAN
FRANK MILL
LEGEND
DARK HORSE COMICS
SIN CITY
6 OF 6
$2.95 US
$4.00 CAN
SIN CIT
A DAME TO KILL F